Shattered Not Broken

A Mother's Journey Through her Daughter's Car Accident and her Son's Suicide

BOBBIE BOMAR BROWN

Copyright©2024 Count Sheep Publishing

ISBN: 978-0-9668622-1-8

All rights reserved. No parts of this publication may be reproduced without prior written permission from the author, bobbiebomarbrown@gmail.com.

Scripture quotations taken from THE HOLY BIBLE, NEW INTERNATIONAL VERSION®. NIV®. Copyright© 1973, 1978, 1984, 2011 by Biblical US, Inc.® Used by permission.

Poems by Robert Kitler, photos of Jennifers accident, and Dr. Barker's quote. Copyright© 2016 Bobbie Bomar Brown. Permission has been granted from all family members mentioned in *Shattered Not Broken*. Recipes are from a lifetime of collecting and from my creations when I owned Bobbie's Catering.

I have depended on my memory, hospital notes and the *Unbreakable Cord* manuscript to write this book. I make no explicit guarantees about the accuracy of the information contained in this book. Names have been changed, except the names of my family, Doctor Barker, and the hospitals. Dialogue is included, but I do not guarantee the exact words, or the order of events are correct.

Cover photo by Tom Swinnen, Pexels photo via Canva.com

Drawing of Woody by Jennifer Kittler

From My Heart

I am deeply grateful for all my friends and family who cried and prayed with me during my daughter's life-threatening car accident twenty-three years ago and the recent heartbreaking loss of my son. Your love and support helped me find the courage to face another day.

My sincere gratitude to the accountant and lawyer for your guidance following the loss of my son. Your compassion was a source of comfort during an incredibly challenging time. Great appreciation for all first responders; your kindness and professionalism meant the world to my family.

A heartfelt thank you to my family, who encouraged me to heal by writing this book, especially my daughter, Jennifer, who walked beside me during the writing and editing process. To Mike, my husband, thank you for giving me the space to heal. A special thanks to my three grandchildren, Logan and his wife Krystin, Emma and Seneca, who shared many brunches with me and gave me a reason to search for more recipes and move forward. And lastly, I dedicate this book to my son, Robert, who gave me so many happy memories to share and silly poems to make me laugh. I will never stop loving you—Shattered, Not Broken.

Table of Contents

Introduction 1

1. The Cry of My Heart 5
2. Shattered 15
3. Ministering Angels 23
4. Silent Tears 33
5. Gods Plans—Satan's Lies 45
6. Terrified 53
7. Split Worlds 65
8. Closed Heart 77
9. The Puzzle 81
10. Straight Edges 87
11. Jen's Final Piece 99
12. Rob's Pieces Wouldn't Fit 115

Through My Eyes: My Son's Verses 119
Treasured Family Recipes 131
Resources 153
Photo Gallery 155
Journal 165

Introduction

"For we are co-workers in God's service, you are God's field, God's building."
1 Corinthians 3:9

    Shattered Not Broken, written as a non-fiction parallel narrative, recounts the medical drama of Jennifer's horrific car accident in 2001 and the death of Robert in 2022. Through the pages you will meet my family and walk with us through laughter and tears.

    I was born on July 7 to Robert and Della Bomar in Fort Worth, Texas. Yes, my legal name is Bobbie, but I was often called Bonnie by people who didn't think Bobbie was a girl's name. Dad gave me the nickname of mouse, and I was called Bobo by my best grade school friend. Mother of two, Jennifer and Robert, grandmother of Logan, Emma and Seneca, Rob's children.

    Collecting recipes and sharing meals with my family holds a special place in my heart. The *Treasured Family Recipes* chapter contains the recipes mentioned in the book, plus a few of our family favorites.

    Jennifer Marie Kittler was born December 7, 1975, in Longmont, Colorado to Bobbie and Gerhard (Gary) Kittler. Named after her maternal grandmother, Della Marie, Jennifer was born on Pearl Harbor Day. My little sunshine, butterfly, buttercup, and Kibbles were her nicknames, but the cutest one was Eyeya, that is what Rob called her when he couldn't pronounce Jennifer. She loves tattoos and has the gift of an encouraging spirit and a thankful heart. She still sends specially designed appreciation cards to her surgeons.

    Robert John Kittler was born July 7, 1977, in Longmont, Colorado, to Bobbie and Gerhard (Gary) Kittler. Robert is named after both his grandfathers, John Kittler and Robert Bomar. Bobbie and Robby share the same birthday. Rob had the gift of making everyone he met feel special. He loved writing poetry and creating acrylic masterpieces. The *Through my Eyes-My Son's Verses* chapter includes Rob's poetry. A funny story about his nicknames is that he was always

Robby, but when he got older, he said, no, it's Rob. Later he answered to Robert, Red Rob was often called Dr. K. as he was only a few credits short of his doctorate in early childhood education. Although, his favorite name was Dad. Father of Logan, Emma, and Seneca. Rob would be so proud of the three of them. In 2024, Logan was among the top 80 to be accepted into the physical therapy doctorate program at the University of Colorado, Anschutz Medical Campus. In August 2024, Emma graduated with a Bachelor of Science in Health Care Management and in October 2024. Seneca graduated from Cosmetology School.

Billy Fred Bomar, my brother, was born on February 24, 1947. He is two years older than me, and he is a key character in this book. His life had a significant impact on my family. In 1987, he sustained a kick to the chest during an altercation outside a California bar, causing his heart to stop. The delay in resuscitating resulted in brain damage. Billy's official diagnosis was hypoxia—a lack of oxygen to the brain cells. He lived twenty-three years as a total care bedridden patient with family members until his death at the age of 67

2021 Covid affected our world like it did to so many others. Billy's daughter, Ashlee, was five at the time of her dad's accident. I became more than an aunt to her, so when Covid took her from us while she was giving birth to her little girl, I was devastated. I found peace in my grief, knowing that she had accepted Christ a few years earlier.

The adventures of Woody weave throughout Jennifer's stories. All fictional dialog from Woody will be noted by the drawing Jennifer drew in the third grade and in italics. Woody was an emotional fictional character in writing my first book, *The Unbreakable Cord.* The actual stuffed dog was purchased in the hospital gift shop and still holds a special place in our hearts. The fluffy stuffed dog sits on my desk as my inspiration and as a reminder of God's mysterious ways.

A previous editor suggested removing his character, as it wasn't necessary to my story. But how could I question God's way of ministering to me? Through the eyes of a fluffy stuffed dog, I found the strength to pen my darkest fears and document the horrific events during Jennifer's 4-month hospital stay. However, now I must find the strength to share this story through my tears.

I will struggle to share this part of my life, but I know to move out of the darkness of my son's death, I must move forward toward the light. I must do it without hiding behind the stuffed dog. During this journey, I am discovering the difference between unbearable pain and unspeakable pain. During Jennifer's horrific accident, at times, the pain was unbearable, but I cried out her injuries. My daily calls to my mother, often choking back my words, I would speak the words: internal decapitation, open book pelvis break, all the many life-threatening issues that threatened her life when the pain became unbearable; I prayed and leaned on God to rescue me.

My son's death is still unspeakable at times. My heart does not want to say the word - suicide. How can I let that word take residence in my heart? Suicide is a hard subject to speak about, and with Jennifer, I held onto hope of her surviving. But Rob's action ripped any chance of a future life with him from my arms. This story will be extremely sad, but this is a story I must share as I know to heal, I need to speak the word suicide. When Rob's story gets too painful, I will share a cute story or a silly poem he wrote for his elementary class.

By sharing our testimonies, we become co-workers with God. The focus switches off us and reminds us that His promises and miracles are real. Stories engage our brains. These events filtered through the fingers of Christ, and I hope that by sharing my journey, you find encouragement in your travels through life and death.

The Unbreakable Cord, written in 2016, is my roadmap for writing *Shattered Not Broken.* Jennifer's stories are shared chronologically, whereas Robert's are interspersed. In re-reading and soaking myself in my experiences, I hope that the words I wrote years ago remain true. I need to prove to myself God is who He says he is, and His promises are true no matter the level of my pain. Believers remind me God's strength will sustain me. Do I really believe this? I made leaning on God sound easy, but my daughter survived the car accident. Would my story have ended the same if she had died that night? Honestly, I do not know. Will my faith be enough to see me through this blanket of sorrow? In my search for answers, I join hands with God and share my story. I must hold tightly to His hands, so I don't slip away as I sort the difficult jigsaw pieces I face today.

Please join hands with us through laughter and tears, breath in each scene as if you were living in that moment, not just reading words on a page. Laugh and cry as we journey together. More importantly, we should see Jesus as the lifeline—a cord that never shatters or breaks.

1

The Cry of My Heart

"Hear my cry, O God, listen to my prayer. From the ends of the earth, I call to you; I call as my heart grows faint; lead me to the rock that is higher than I. For you have been my refuge, a strong tower against the foe."
Psalm 61:1-3

24 November 2001~Recounts the events of Jennifer's accident. Awakened by the ringing of my cell phone, Rob quickly spoke, saying that Jennifer had been in a car accident. After giving me the hospital details, I headed to Aurora, Colorado, a two-hour drive. I met Rob and Gary, Jen's dad, in the trauma waiting room.

A young physician stepped forth and said, "Mr. and Mrs. Kittler." I had not answered that name since our divorce twenty years earlier and did not find it necessary to correct him. We listened as he shared the news concerning our daughter.

"The lacerated kidney isn't a huge concern at this point as it will repair itself. The head gash required twenty-seven staples to close. The multiple pelvic fractures are our main concern." He then continued with a slight hesitation, "It is a deep bleeder, and your daughter has already lost a lot of blood. We inserted a central venous catheter to speed up the blood transfusions."

The nurse directed us to her triage room, swallowing the knot in my throat, "Jennifer." Holding her pale hand in mine— "Do you remember what happened?"

She spoke in a girlish voice that was unknown to me. Her colorless face rendered a weak smile, and she whispered,

"Thanksgiving at your house. Walmart's Black Friday. Never will I do that for a three-dollar toaster." With slurred speech, she continued. "I remember leaving this morning after Weight Watchers, and then I met up with my friends. Are they hurt? What happened?"

Jennifer slipped her fingers between her neck and the thick collar and said, "This hurts. Why do I have it on? I need to go to the bathroom." She talked without catching her breath and did not wait for an answer concerning her friends.

The attending nurse reminded her the cervical collar was standard procedure for rear-end collisions and that she couldn't get up. While the nurse scooped Jennifer's bloody clothes from the floor, I noticed piles of my daughter's beautiful auburn hair strewn around.

Once again, Jennifer begged to go to the bathroom.

"You cannot get up, but you do have a urinary catheter in place," the nurse firmly said while preparing her for the CT scan. She removed my daughter's neck, tongue, and ear piercings and then said, "Looks like you enjoy tattoos."

A smile filled her pale face, and her silliness continued. Because of the late hour, the doctor allowed us into the viewing room. The technician spoke softly, "Jennifer, lie still. Do not move."

Girlishly, she said, "Okay." Nevertheless, the fixation of the lighted oxygen meter on her finger overrode his instructions. The small light found its new home inches from her eyes.

The nurse who had removed her piercings slipped on a lead vest and stood near her head. He constantly whispered, "Jennifer, don't move."

"Finished," the doctor spoke through the intercom. "Get her to intensive care." He pointed at the computer on the desk. "Mr. and Mrs. Kittler, let me show you what I see. There is a thin shadow around the top neck disc, the C1. I do not think it's a concern. Discs are like pretzels: if they crack, they break, and I do not see a break."

Why does she keep asking to pee and waving her hands?"

He interrupted me before I could ask about brain damage. "I know you have lots of questions. The strange behavior could be from heavy medication or trauma. Mrs. Kittler, you do know that the first responders used the Jaws of Life to free your daughter. The car was a tangled mess. The next twelve hours are crucial. Let's get her through them, and then we'll schedule the pelvis surgery."

Gary and I rejoined the family in the narrow hall and shared everything the doctor had said. Rob said to the nurse, "I've noticed two police officers here the entire time. What's with that?" The nurse informed us the drunk driver sustained minor injuries and would be arrested when released.

My son and his wife, Melissa, enclosed me in their arms, and their kisses lingered. I didn't want to let go of their embrace.

2018~The world I knew would soon change. Rob mentioned experiencing dizzy spells when getting off the sofa. My first thought was low blood sugar. I suggested he make an appointment with his doctor. We had just returned from Arizona for the summer, and thinking nothing more about it, we went to Longmont for groceries. Juggling bags of toiletries, I managed to answer my cell phone; it was Emma, my oldest granddaughter. I could tell by her voice something was wrong.

"Grandma! Dad is in the hospital; they think he is having a heart attack."

"Slow down, Emma, and tell me what hospital he is in. We will meet you there."

With supplies thrown in the car, we drove forty-five minutes to the hospital. A volunteer directed us to his room; I knew then it wasn't a heart attack as they didn't send us to the Intensive care area.

His girls, Emma and Seneca, snuggled tightly on each side of him. His oldest, Logan, stood bedside. Rob always put his kids first, and today was no different. He reassured them he would be fine, and it was nothing to worry about. Rob explained that he had driven himself to the emergency room when he started dropping things and couldn't walk straight. They rushed him to the trauma unit, thinking he was having a heart attack.

After the brain scan, blood work, and EKG, we were waiting for the doctor to explain the results. None of us were prepared for the news. Looking directly at Rob, the doctor said, "The scan shows a brain tumor, hemangioblastoma, but not cancerous. This causes tumors throughout the body, and further testing will need to be done to see if it is Von Hipple-Lindau Syndrome then, all your kids will have to be evaluated as this is a hereditary disease. However, now we need to remove the tumor as it is pressing on your brain stem."

"Why didn't I take his concern more seriously? Rob never complains about being sick; I should have realized it was something more than low blood sugar". How I wished it had been news of a heart attack or a bad case of indigestion. The doctor said surgery is scheduled for Wednesday, and Rob will go home on Friday; it made it sound so simple. But how could we not worry when thinking of removing part of his skull to get to the brain tumor?

With Jennifer's care, I never doubted anything the doctors said or questioned their plan. Her doctors were so caring and informative. So, I trusted them. I took this same mindset with Rob's doctor. Now, I wish I had asked more questions, but I was struggling to process what was really happening to my son. I had never heard of hemangioblastoma.

Mike and I checked into the hotel across from the hospital and made the necessary phone calls, notifying friends and asking for prayers.

Another precious life from God was in jeopardy, and my world was shattered once again.

2001~The pain medication finally subdued the girlish Jennifer. The cold intensive care unit matched my lonely heart, and the smell of the disinfectant hurled me back fourteen years to the California trauma unit, where my brother, Billy, battled for his life. The family was faced with the heartbreaking decision of removing his life support.

"Good morning, Mrs. Kittler," jolted me to the current situation I was facing. "Jennifer remains stable. One of the best orthopedic surgeons in the area will be performing her pelvis surgery tomorrow morning. I've ordered another blood transfusion." Stepping outside, I asked him about brain damage. "Too early to tell. With the high-speed rear-end impact your daughter endured, it's lucky that she survived. Let's focus on one thing at a time. She isn't out of the woods. Please go home and get some rest."

I can't believe he expects me to leave. I replied as nicely as I could. "Thank you for your concern."

The teeter-totter movement of Jen's hand started once again as soon as she awoke. The light rested inches from her eyes. The nurse removed the oxygen meter from her finger and said, "Jennifer, let's move this to your toe. You'll rest better." With the offending light motionless, my daughter drifted back to sleep.

Gary and his wife, Karen, arrived around eight in the morning. Glancing at Jen's IV pole, Gary said, "I know the doctor said the pelvis was a deep bleeder, but you would think that she'd have a little color with all of the blood transfusions."

"I know. The nurse said she was on her ninth unit."

Exhaustion tugged at me, so Gary dropped me off at the closest motel. After a brief nap, I returned to the hospital and to reality. The orthopedic doctor was in her room, and he said, "Because it's an open-book pelvis break, I'll be screwing a small metal plate onto the pubic bone and pulling the pelvis back together. Surgery is scheduled for nine a.m. tomorrow."

"Will she walk again?" her dad asked.

"I'm sorry, I can't guarantee anything; time and rehab will give us the answers. I will see you in the morning." His firm handshake was comforting.

Helplessness covered me in the quietness of Jen's room while I watched my sleeping beauty. Seeing her hands restricted, my heart cried, but when they were free, she pulled her chest tubes. She's so different when she's awake—she's giddy and even silly at times. I hope it's the medication.

As nurses bathed Jennifer, I went to the coffee shop; this little furry stuffed dog caught my eye or was it the 'on sale' that grabbed my attention? Returning to her room, a technician standing over her said. "Open wide; Doctor Barker wants a picture looking through your mouth." As he pulled the cylinder away, he said, "Thanks, Jen. You did great."

I haven't met Doctor Barker, and I wonder who he is. I laid the stuffed dog on my daughter's tummy, "Look what I got from the gift shop. Isn't he cute? Can you think of a name?"

"Woody, Woody. He looks like Woody," the girlish voice said.

"A black-and-white spotted dog doesn't look like a Woody, but since he's yours, Woody, it will be." Untying her hands from the bed rails. Jennifer giggled and embraced her new friend. Immediately, she lifted him in the air; I stood there, ready to retrieve her wandering hands.

Jennifer's nurse placed her hand on my shoulder; it was the lightest of touches, "Mrs. Kittler, the doctor, called. The pelvis surgery is canceled. Dr. Barker, the spine surgeon, will explain everything. In the meantime, he ordered Jennifer's bed to be lowered and remain flat —no movement at all." The nurse slowly lowered the head of Jen's bed and restrained her hands. The recliner caught my shaking body. Racing thoughts filled my mind, " Please explain why the spine doctor? What did the X-ray through the mouth show?

My little music director's hands were once again confined to the Finally, a young, handsome doctor entered the room wearing a starched white medical jacket." I wanted to ask about his credentials, but I could not form the words. "I am Doctor Barker, a spine surgeon. Sorry, it took so long. What I saw on the x-ray is exceedingly rare, and I wanted my findings confirmed. Your daughter's neck ligaments are torn, and her skull is being held in place by a thin thread. The injury is called 'occipital-cervical dislocation, which is often known as 'internal decapitation."

He continued explaining that internal decapitation is rare; the skull separates from the spinal column, which is usually fatal. "She ruptured the ligaments that connect her neck to her head. I know this is overwhelming, but we must act quickly to stabilize the neck. I've scheduled a cervical halo team to place her in a cervical vest/brace. This will immobilize her neck and protect her spine. They will secure the halo with pins through Jennifer's scalp and slightly into her skull. Mrs. Kittler, I know this is a lot of information, but this needs to be done. You know the pelvis surgery is canceled, but the pelvis must be stabilized before we can sit her up and attach the halo. The orthopedic doctor will explain that procedure.

Information kept coming at me; all I could do was nod and trust Doctor Barker. I was thankful Gary, Karen, and Rob were now here with me as the orthopedic doctor explained how the outside fixator to secure her pelvis worked. "My team will use a self-drilling screw on each side of her pelvis. Two sliding link rods on the outside will meet in the middle and attach to each other, tightening and securing the pelvis. The two screws will fixate the sacroiliac joint." As the orthopedic doctor finished explaining the procedure, a representative from the cervical halo team stepped forth and began explaining the halo vest. He showed us each piece of hardware and talked as if he were selling a nice set of cookware. He handed Gary the manufacturer's booklet and informed us when the pelvis was stabilized; his medical team would deaden the four pin sites before they screw them into the skull.

We weren't allowed to stay and were told both procedures would take an hour, so we gathered in the waiting room. "Did he really say, 'screws into her skull?'" Running my fingers through my hair, a nervous habit I could never shake, and sat numb as Gary nodded.

I related the horrific details to my mother. I cleared the lump from my throat. "Mom, it missed her spinal cord by less than a millimeter, and the doctor said that she will need neck surgery, and she'll never drive again because the hardware implanted will prevent her from turning her neck. She's listed as critical now." She waited for my crying to stop, then reminded me that I was strong and that I should not forget to lean on God. Saying our goodbyes, I rushed back to the waiting room.

"Mr. and Mrs. Kittler, they're finished. You can go in."

Rob steadied me as we both stood bedside; my trembling hands enclosed her pale hand. My giddy Jennifer was gone, and hideous metal bars outlined her tear-stained face. I didn't have the heart to look under the sheet that now covered bars protruding from her pale body. Her vacant eyes stared into space as if she were searching for relief. God's indwelling strength overrode the unbearable pain in my heart, and faint words surfaced. "Sweetheart, it's Mom and Rob. Your dad and Karen are also here. We love you so much."

2018~Robert's doctor explained the procedure once again, assuring us he would have a computerized roadmap to locate the tumor. Again, he reconfirmed surgery on Wednesday, and Rob would be able to go home on Friday, so no particular care would be needed.

When the word cancer was taken out of the diagnosis, we were relieved but numb. His dad nor I asked questions. Flashes of Billy's closed brain injury attacked me and reminded me how fragile the brain is. The thought of cutting into layers of the brain to remove the tumor scared me, and I am sure it scared Rob, too.

The girls snuggled up beside their dad in the small bed until the nurses prepped him for surgery. Rob joked about his little blue bouffant hat. He was an expert at keeping his feelings hidden from all of us. A calmness filled his façade, trying to reassure us things would be okay.

Family filled Rob's room; this time, Jennifer stood beside her brother. As we held hands, I prayed. I remember struggling with the words of my prayer and can't recall what I prayed, but I will never forget my son's face as he looked up at me and said, "Thank you, Mom."

Directed to the surgical waiting room, each of us found our spot. Gary worked on crossword puzzles, and I began updating the prayer chain. Logan sat at the counter and did homework. The girls went to the mall. I have spent too much of my life in hospital waiting rooms; I wonder if I have angered Christ that He keeps placing me in these cold, scary places. Everyone looks at me like a strong person; it is Jesus preventing me from breaking. Although it still would be nice to have a hug from my mama— she died in 2004. Being strong is a lonely place.

The wait seemed forever before the nurse escorted us to an undecorated conference room. Before the surgeon sat down, he commented it was a difficult tumor to reach but reassured us the surgery was successful. I sensed something didn't go as planned. It was as if a bomb dropped and silenced the room. As he explained the tumor, the brain mapping didn't work, and it was hard to reach the tumor. He explained the tumor was enclosed in a cyst, and when they popped the cyst, the tumor moved and was pushed up next to the cerebellum. He continued telling us it was difficult to remove. I have heard many doctors trying to explain mistakes, and I really felt someone had made a mistake during his surgery. Although, I know time would tell the truth. I had sat bedside during Jennifer's life-threatening emergencies, but my heart was telling me something wasn't right with my son's surgery.

It seemed forever before I was able to see my son in ICU. I reached for his hand and softly said, Mom is here; love you, and before I could say anymore, the nurse whispered, "Didn't they explain brain surgery recovery details?"

She further said, "Your son's brain is trying to process. He has a sheet over him; please do not talk or touch him.

I sat helpless by my little Robby; my heart cried to my heavenly Father for strength.

2
Shattered

*"We are hard pressed on every side, but not crushed, perplexed,
but not in despair, persecuted, but not abandoned, struck down,
but not destroyed."*
2 Corinthians 4:8-9

2001~Thankfully, the nurse rolled in a recliner to Jennifer's room. The heated blanket lightly covered my exhausted body until a whisper woke me up, "Mrs. Kittler, I know it's late, but the doctor ordered an MRI to check the alignment of Jennifer's halo.

Securing the portable heart monitor and all the IV poles, Jennifer tightly cringed to Woody as One of the aides guided the headboard, and the other placed both hands on the footboard and pulled the bed down the cold, empty hall. Half walking and half running, I struggled to keep up with their young pace. Jen's nurse did not miss a beat. They delivered their cargo to the waiting attendant. Immediately, Jennifer's pale body shook as if volts of electricity had entered her. Drooling dripped down her cheeks.

Jen knocked Woody to the floor. "Jennifer, Jennifer," the nurse yelled and pushed me. "Mrs. Kittler, please leave." Picking Woody up off the floor, I left my daughter against my wishes. More nurses rushed in.

Propped up against the wall, sitting on the floor, trying to remain calm. I pulled my knees to my chest, rocking back and forth, praying that she hadn't died. My heart pounded against Woody's soft body; I was prepared for the worst.

Mrs. Kittler, Jennifer is stable. She had a stroke. The on-call neurologist is on his way from his home. You can see her now."

I skimmed my hand over her cold, stiff arm. "Jennifer, it's Mom. I am right here, honey." I tried comforting her with my words, but her loud cries overrode my voice. "The doctor still wants the MRI; you must calm down." I placed her new companion under her lifeless left arm and kissed her cold, spongy cheek. The attendants transferred her onto the small exam table. Jennifer calmed down as a sedative flowed through her IV tube.

She slipped into the MRI tube before they made me leave.

"Mrs. Kittler, while we wait for the doctor, do you want some coffee? It is already Tuesday morning, and I know you haven't slept much the last couple of days," Jen's nurse said.

"I would love a Dr Pepper if you can find one this early." The cold Dr Pepper refreshed my dry throat, and the handshake of the neurologist eased my jitteriness.

"Your daughter did have a stroke. Her left side is paralyzed, but her face has regained some sensitivity. I have scheduled many tests for her this morning. The results will show the cause and the exact location of the stroke." He paused and then said, "And the severity of the brain damage."

The nurse handed me a warm blanket and escorted me to the conference room. "It's more comfortable." Gary and Karen joined me. Magazine after magazine filled the long nine hours, and the silence stretched until the doctor entered the room and spoke. "The high-speed rear-end impact caused a small tear in her carotid artery. A blood clot broke free and traveled to her brain. I'm so sorry. I know you received shocking news about the C1 fracture. The orthopedic surgeon needs to fix her pelvis, and the spine surgeon needs to repair her neck. I am now in charge of your daughter's care. I am her gatekeeper, all surgeries are canceled until I approve them."

Gary said, "What about brain damage?"

"It's too early to know. The right side of the brain controls the left side of the body. Her ability to process new information may suffer, as the interruption of blood flow affected her new-learning region."

💔

2018~Rob's craniotomy surgery, the procedure involved making an incision in the scalp and removing a piece of the bone from the skull to give the neurosurgeon access to the tumor. Rob's incision required twenty non-dissolvable sutures to replace the bone.

My heart broke seeing Rob scared and not knowing what to say. His doctor was not very encouraging, as I felt they were avoiding telling us something. The first night, the surgeon didn't even come to check on Rob; he sent his assistant.

When questioning, the reason Rob struggle to see or why he felt as if a light was always on in his brain, our questions went unanswered. The strange comment from the PA sent a chill up my spine. "We didn't do anything that would affect his sight."

While he was sitting on his bedside, My heart ached as I watched him struggling to button his shirt. He couldn't even walk without stumbling. Now, the doctor says Rob would need to relearn some basic things that the brain just automatically does; this wasn't mentioned before surgery as a potential side effect.

His medical team washed their hands of Rob's issues by insisting he go to the rehab facility where they could help with his balance and basic self-care. Recalling the wonderful work Craig rehab did for my broken daughter, I wanted my son to have that help. I was instrumental in him going. That is one of many regrets I have concerning Rob's recovery.

The location of the facility was convenient, and it was a beautiful facility. However, it wasn't anything like Craig's rehab; it had the feeling of a nursing home. Rob was only thirty-nine and surrounded by older, frail patients.

One of my favorite photos of him as a toddler sits on my bookcase; I can't help but smile when I reflect on it. My little Robby needed hernia surgery, and, in the seventies, patients had to check in the hospital the night before. He wasn't sick or feeling bad, so keeping

17

an active two-year-old in his room was impossible. He would walk up and down the hall in his little white hospital gown; he was so cute. Occasionally, older patients smiled at him and talked to him, and he would walk into their room. Thankfully, we were on the floor where older patients were hospitalized for minor checkups. The nurse said his little smile was one of their best therapies.

But that isn't the case at the rehab facility; no one smiled at him or spoke, and they were all in their own world trying to heal themselves. This environment made Rob's recovery extra hard; he needed his kids and pets surrounding him. We realized we had to focus on his mental recovery more than the physical. It was just too hard emotionally for him to stay. We checked him out after five days.

As a single dad, he had lots of responsibilities and didn't really like asking for help. He was dedicated to his children and needed that interaction. Rob loved cats; he got his first cat, Pope, when he was in high school. He made a little catwalk above the windows, stretching halfway around the room. Later, Paige replaced Pope. He trained Paige to fetch a glitter pom pom ball as he threw it up the handmade ramp. Rob spoiled Paige, and she was his companion for many years

At the time of the surgery, Rob was working in a tourist town at the local hotel as a ghost tour guide, and they didn't offer insurance. Rob said he felt nudged to apply for Medicaid, and this was a couple of days before going to the emergency room. The case worker was great. She got him enrolled at once and, in the following months, continued to ensure Rob and the children had all the services they needed.

We were shocked but not surprised by the news from Rob's new primary doctor. In reviewing Rob's latest brain scan, he pointed to a spot on the monitor and said, "They nicked the cerebellum while removing the tumor. Rob, the cerebellum controls balance for walking and standing and other complex motor functions. I can see why you have the issues you have now."

We knew with this information that the lost part of the cerebellum couldn't magically be replaced, and that Rob's brain would need to compensate. I believe that day; the devil got a huge foothold on Rob because I noticed he became more anxious and fearful.

Estes Park had wonderful home health care, and we even had some of the nurses who assisted with Billy's care. Rob responded to physical therapy and began regaining his balance. Occupational therapy helped with simple things like buttoning his shirt. We found an eye doctor who specialized in brain injuries and helped with his vision and light sensitivity. We rarely saw Rob without a pair of sunglasses, and he kept his house dark.

Making the most of his temporary need for the wheelchair, Rob rolled around the kitchen, preparing his famous breakfast burritos and bacon for his kids. They call them 'Rob burritos.' The Rob burrito recipe isn't included in the recipe chapter, which was something special he did for his kids. I never had the recipe. Once, he included a hundred-dollar bill in each of their foil-wrapped burritos. Rob loved grilling steak, ordering BBQ, or spreading cream cheese on a bagel for his kids.

Rob pushed himself, trying to regain what the damaged cerebellum had taken away. We were praying the changes were only temporary. But the physical challenges were not what drained him; the fear of the unknown assaulted him.

After surgery, he shared how little things overwhelmed him. It was common for him to tell me how he had trouble focusing and processing information. I wished I had truly understood what he meant when he said, "I just want to feel normal again." How long did the thought of dying haunt him? All of us tried our hardest to encourage him that everything would improve, but I am sure he didn't believe us. Rob rarely expressed his fears, but looking back, so much more had to be stressing him; he just never shared.

Even in his struggles, he thought of others. Rob would send all of us funny emojis. Mine and Jennifer's are the ones with dark glasses on. I see my son's smiling face every time I see that one. I still have the funniest drawing that he tacked on my bulletin board—a little stick man with the saying 'I am under attack.'

I began handling the doctor's appointments, his insurance and financial paperwork. Rob and I faced reality quickly and knew returning to work would be impossible. Together, we gathered all the needed information, and I completed the application for Social Security disability. Friends told him Social Security never approved your first request. Money was tight; even if approved, we knew the money wouldn't start right away. This only added to his stress. Rob made the first phone visit with the Social Security Administration and then gave me permission to act for him. I corresponded with her weekly; she was the most amazing and helpful person. Finally, after tons of paperwork, many phone calls and meetings with their disability doctors, he was approved. Such a huge pressure lifted off us. Working as a tour guide, gratuities made up a part of his income, and social security checks didn't equal his income. Rob hated depending on others, so he sold his canoe, paddle boards and anything else that would bring him a little extra money.

2001~Jennifer's many life-threatening injuries complicated her medical treatment. So, the decision was made to place her in a medicated coma. The fear of another blood clot breaking loose, they couldn't chance surgery. Plus, this would also help with pain management. Doctor Jones placed his hand on my shoulder and softly said, "Mrs. Kittler, you must go home and get some rest." I managed a small nod. He was right; my heavy eyes won the battle. Gary dropped me off at the closest motel. Because of my poor vision, I had to depend on friends and family to drive me. I was thankful that Gary and his wife, Karen, could sit with Jennifer; I didn't want her to be alone. In my loneliness, I depended on my Savior.

28 November 2001~Tthree days since the call that shook my world, but it feels like months since I was home decorating for Christmas. After a few hours of rest, I returned to my caged daughter.

"Mrs. Kittler, the doctor needs to check Jennifer's brain functions. I know you hate seeing her in pain, but this is the window for peeking into her brain."

Once her restraints had been untied and the flow of the white liquid had stopped, the gatekeeper stood at the foot of her bed. He recited his routine script. "Jennifer, Jennifer, push your right foot against my hand as if you were pressing a gas pedal good. Now, push your left foot. Push harder harder." He moved to her bedside and picked up her right hand. "Squeeze my hand harder. Good." He reached across her body and repeated the same commands for her left hand. Then he shook his head and said, "Nothing today from the left side, but maybe tomorrow."

Jen's right arm swung sporadically; Woody flew over the bed rail. "Jennifer! You cannot pull on the IVs," the nurse said as she restrained the wild hand.

The doctor advised us each time the medication was turned off to reassure her of where she was. My message confessing our love for her and that she had been in a car accident and was in the hospital was delivered before the milky sedative returned her to the medicated coma. As I continued, the monotonous opening and closing of her clenched hand gave me purpose. I prayed that life would return to her frozen side.

2001~Rob and his wife, Melissa, were supportive while Jennifer was in the hospital. My son's smile always warmed my heart, and I recall this one day special when he came to the hospital; he uncovered his sister's feet, speaking in a soft voice expressing his love; he painted her toenails purple, her favorite color. Melissa set a poster board on the foot of Jen's bed and said, "We made this for you. I know you can't see it, but I hope you can hear me. It's a beautiful collage filled with pictures of your family. And this beautiful poem Rob wrote. Of course, I included photos of Slippers. Logan feeds him daily."

Robs sensitive heart. carried a talent for writing poetry that he loved sharing. Clearing the lump from his throat, he knelt at Jen's bedside and read his Poem.

A Miracle Named Jen

As you lay there, you rest,
As we all seem to look.
You were on a quest,
Counting calories, you would cook!
We all are so confused,
Dazed: not knowing what's true.
How can I help you?
What can I do?
I see you smile; yes, I do.
I know it hurts; it hurts me too.
Just last night, I cried to you.
Praying for you is all I can do.
What happened to you,
It is not a choice you would ever choose.
To God we pray every day for you.
Doctors, nurses, and family, too.
Even God is resonating with you.
Jen, you've got to pull through,
Because in life, you've got so much to do:
Flowers to smell
And cards that say, "get well."
The family you need, Slippers to feed,
Piercings might bleed,
Bandages you'll need.
A smile to show to the people you know
And blessings as you grow—
As your heart begins to glow.
Stay with us, Jen.
I know how hard it's been.
For in your life, this is when
Ups and downs
And rights and wrongs
It is only going to make you strong.
Some battles, you'll lose,
But this one, you'll win.
Because no one can fill the shoes
Of a miracle sister named Jen.

3
Ministering Angels

*"For he will command his angels concerning you to guard you in
all your ways; they will lift you up in their hands so that you will
not strike your foot against a stone."*
Psalm 91:11-12

2001~Jennifer fought the soft straps that held her prisoner, and Woody flew through the air, landing on the end of the bed. I swear Woody knew when Jennifer's pain peaked. Was he alerting me to the fact that Jennifer needed help? I retrieved him and whispered into his floppy ear. "I know that one day, we will laugh at the things she did when they turned off the mother's milk. The funniest story happened when the hospital chaplain stopped in as Jennifer pulled on her nightgown, exposing bare breasts—his face turned beat red, and his chin quivered." I can't believe I am talking to a stuffed dog, and worse, I think he giggled. Sleep deprivation does weird things. Escaping into a fantasy world was my way of surviving. The nurse was quickly informed of Jen's erratic behavior. The battle with the restraints ended when the increase in pain medication reached its destination.

"Every time the doctor called, the gatekeeper comes in and turns off the sedative pump; I can see how it hurts Bobbie, especially saying good-bye to her daughter as she drifted away, but seeing the immense pain Jennifer was suffering shattered Bobbie's heart."

At evening rounds, Doctor Barker explained the neck surgery. "She'll have two titanium rods screwed to both sides of her spine and then fused to her C4. Then a smaller rod running perpendicular to that one will be attached to the middle of her skull and screwed into it."

I watched as he sketched little lines on his pad. My mind's eye saw a ticktacktoe game that was missing the bottom line. Although I knew that it wasn't a game, he continued to explain the procedure. "We'll harvest bone from her hip and fuse it C 4 to skull bone for extra reinforcement and permanent support."

30 November 2001~Gary's boss understood the severity of Jen's accident and allowed him a flexible schedule. Daily, he sat at her bedside while I was taking a lunch break. Our high school marriage had ended twenty years ago. Despite our differences, we came together for our daughter. After making all the necessary phone calls and devouring a grilled cheese sandwich, I returned and found my home on her left side. Gary always positioned himself on the right side of her bed. We worked as a team; while I opened and closed her clenched fist, he found his purpose, waving his crossword puzzle magazine across her heated face.

2022~I will never accept the thought Rob wanted to die, but I do believe he wanted to escape the intense pain and despair he was in. God provided a stuffed dog, Woody, when my heart was shattered. Journaling was my escape from the fear of losing my daughter. Twenty-two years later, God provided me with another escape, a ministering angel came in the form of Transient Global Amnesia. That is what my therapist called it, but I know it was a ministering angel sent to carry me and shelter me from the events of that chilly night. I don't know a lot of the details of what all happened to me, only bits and pieces of what my family has shared. Everyone agreed it best, I don't know. One thing my daughter did say was I kept asking for Gary and wouldn't believe he had died nine months earlier. Of course, this is only a guess, but my mind must have been searching for the teammate I had during our daughter's crisis. I knew I wasn't going to be the strong one this time.

Did my ministering angel protect me or anchor me to this unspeakable pain? Transient Global amnesia, or shock, whatever it was and still is, I know I am frozen in this state I do not like. I try to move forward, but acceptance hasn't reached my heart. Can I emerge shattered, not broken?

Rob was a believer, and the devil must have painted him such a picture of despair that it overrode God, telling Rob he was perfectly made and loved.

I don't have a little stuffed dog helping me process this nightmare, so I must stay strong and attempt to search for answers. Although I have accepted that I will never see my son again, when I see a young man wearing a sweatshirt and sunglasses walking down the street, I still do a double take. Seneca and I have this saying, "My mind knows he's gone, but my heart looks for him in everything."

3 December 2001~At, five Thirty in the Morning, I received a call from the hospital saying Jennifer had had another stroke, so I headed back to the hospital as quickly as I could.

"How bad was this stroke? Will she recover?"

The doctor's face looked apologetic, "I'm sorry, Mrs. Kittler I think it was a mini stroke, but it's too early to know the damage. We'll keep Jennifer on the ventilator in the medicated coma. I canceled the neck surgery."

I refreshed my coffee and made the needed phone calls before returning to Jen's bedside. Please, dear God, let my voice keep my precious daughter connected to this world. I grabbed Woody, found my bookmark on Charlotte's Web, and began reading.

The evening shift change greeted Jennifer with a new bag of dark-red blood. I watched as it dripped through the tiny plastic tubing and into her chest port. Suddenly, her body jumped and jerked—her hands fought the restraints. A loud alarm filled her room, and nurses rushed to her bedside. Monitors flashed her heart rate, 160, and her blood pressure, 186. Then, there was a firm push on my shoulder. "Move! You need to leave," the nurse said.

My book fell and hit the floor, but I caught Woody in midair. Jesus, please help me. I can't do this alone. You've protected her so far—please don't let her die. The cold stucco wall in the hall supported my weeping body. Amazingly, whenever Jennifer had an emergency, and I was asked to step outside her room, this stranger or an encourager sent by God walked by on his way to visit his son. Confiding that his son has been in intensive care for over a month, and it's a long and draining journey, so I need to take care of myself. I don't think I ever told him how his simple hello or just a smile encouraged me. His son died years later from complications from brain surgery, and his son's life led to a Colorado State Law on medical transparency.

"Bobbie, you can come back in. We have her stabilized; the numbers are good, and her blood pressure has fallen. It was a reaction to the blood transfusion. She's already had multiple transfusions, and her immune system produces antibodies to destroy the donor blood."

The nurse who had pushed me earlier continued to speak in a soft voice. "We must give her this unit of blood, and the doctor has another unit scheduled for midnight. We gave her Benadryl, and that will help. I know you want to spend the night, but you must take care of yourself. We'll take care of your daughter."

"Jennifer, it's Mom. I don't know if you can hear me, but I've tucked Woody under your arm. He'll stay with you while I get some sleep. Love you. I'll see you first thing in the morning." I called for a taxi. I was a little sick of everyone telling me what I needed. I wanted to be with my daughter, but once again, I folded. Then I remembered the encouraging words from the stranger who had been living his nightmare for over a month. I knew I did need to take care of myself.

My pillow didn't bring me the comfort I sought. My mind replayed the recent words of the doctor: "I don't know if she'll walk again. She'll never drive again. Too early to know if there's any brain damage." Words from my past also confronted me. I heard my spiritual mentor ask, "Bobbie, what do you want from your walk with God?" My reply— "I want to model my dependency on Him as my total care brother is dependent on others"—also haunted me.

I wondered if I was a hypocrite. Could I really surrender and depend on God for all my needs? It was easy to confess my faith in Christ, but now I had to live it minute by minute. I was afraid, and my faith was all that I had left. I wondered whether it would be enough. My courage and strength are fading.

The following morning, the doctor viewed Jennifer's medical notes; his silence tugged on my heart until he finally spoke, "She's been on the ventilator for forty-eight hours, and the chance of pneumonia is high. Because of the cervical halo, the nurses can't rotate her enough to keep her lungs cleared. Let's give her twenty-four hours, and then we'll reevaluate the surgery. Continue talking to her; the Van Morrison music is great, and the purple toenail polish is awesome. I know this is hard for you, Mrs. Kittler, but your daughter is a fighter; she's fought every battle thrown at her. I'll see you during my evening rounds. I asked my mom to include Jennifer in her prayer chain."

I updated Gary with the newest information. We resumed our daily routine. He took his place on Jennifer's right side and read aloud the daily happenings from the local newspaper. I returned to my recliner and slowly opened and closed her clenched fist. An ear-piercing sound filled the room. Jennifer's pale body jerked and rose inches off the bed. Her room filled with nurses who shouted for us to leave.

"I was scared when the nurse yelled, 'Hand me the Ambu bag.' She covered my sweet Jenny's mouth and kept squeezing the red ball until the other nurse reconnected the hose to the big machine. I learned the difference between the alarms that day. A low, steady beep called attention to an empty medication bag; the nurses would come in to fix that whenever it fit their schedule. On the night of Jenny's reaction to the blood transfusion, the monitors flashed, and the alarm didn't compete to be heard. But when the hose popped off, there was a sound like a fire alarm screaming now! Her parents didn't speak of the incident; they both returned to their original spaces. Gary continued reading the newspaper as if nothing had disturbed him.

Bobbie pulled out her spiral notebook and wiped the dew from her eyes as she wrote in her little notebook."

5 December 2001~Evening rounds brought light into the darkness, and the gatekeeper said, "Mr. and Mrs. Kittler, Jennifer's CT scan looks good. I didn't see any blood clots. I'll inform Doctor Barker he can schedule the neck surgery."

During early morning rounds, Dr. Barker said, "Good—all of you are here. Her neck surgery is scheduled for Tuesday, December eleventh. I want to go over the surgery with you both again."

Two titanium bars, screws and harvested bone, these unfamiliar words would become part of Jennifer's identity forever. Every question her dad asked was answered. Gary had a way of thinking with his head and not letting his emotions control him.

I asked, "Have you ever done this surgery before?"

His truthful answer softly flowed from his young, handsome face. "No, I haven't. Most patients don't survive a high-speed rear-end impact like the one Jennifer experienced. I have performed many surgeries on the C1 and below. I'll have an experienced team of doctors aiding me. She will do fine with the surgery. Please remember that she won't be able to turn her neck, which will prevent her from driving. Any more questions?"

Gary asked how long his daughter would need to keep the halo on. "A few months to stabilize the neck while it heals."

Gary and I simultaneously said, "Thank you, Doctor Barker."

7 December 2001~Jennifer remained sedated on her 26th birthday, so her Aunt Goody and I took a birthday cake to the trauma unit. Thank you for giving Jennifer her twenty-sixth birthday and surrounded with purple flowers decorated the sheet cake.

Gary slid open the glass doors and joined me in her birthday celebration, his tear-glazed eyes focused on the words of the birthday card he read to her. He kissed his daughter's cheek and whispered Happy birthday.

The respiratory therapist said, "Jen's lungs are diminished, and she has a low-grade temperature, so I've ordered a rotational therapy bed that will rotate her from side to side. She's been on the ventilator for seven days; we don't want pneumonia."

7 July 1977~Robert's first birthday made the news; the only baby born in Longmont on 7-7-77. Another fun tidbit is that he was also born on my birthday. I have shared 45 years of birthday celebrations with my son. Pizza places, Estes Park go-carts, water skiing at Horse Tooth Reservoir and backyard picnics.

Rob, my youngest, was always my little rescuer. Making people feel special and loved came so naturally to him. I once read that when a child is born on their mother's birthday, they have a spiritual bond, and I find that to be true. One of my most treasured gifts from him is a poem he wrote for my birthday, *Tribute To Mom;* you will find it in the special chapter *Through My Eyes My Son's Verses.*

Rob's care and love extended to his disabled uncle Billy. After Mama's death in 2004, Rob and I became Billy's court-approved guardians. In 2008, Robert moved to Estes Park so he could help with Billy's care. All of us as a family remodeled our detached four-car garage into a small apartment. Rob never complained about his accommodation, or the work and commitment Billy required

April 2024~I began this writing journey of *Shattered Not Broken* with the purpose of thanking God for my children and grandchildren. I write to heal and move forward to honor Rob's life. Also, as a reminder for my daughter that the actions of the drunk driver didn't ruin her life; it only changed. I must focus on those words and believe with Rob's death; my life is forever changed but not ruined.

Nothing will take away the pain in my heart; the shattered line can't be refilled. To keep my heart from breaking, I bravely move forward. I can't express strongly enough how powerful the word "bravely" is here. Painful memories surface without warning, and I often find myself scared to look, but I bravely slowly move through that painful memory, and then I find a glimmer of light in a funny story or a poem my son wrote.

2018~We were not prepared for the changes that removing his brain tumor placed in our path. We didn't realize it was going to be a long and heartbreaking journey. The doctor made everything sound simple, but it was far from simple.

I love nurturing my children, but during their traumatic time, both needed me in separate ways. I was encouraged to touch Jennifer, read to her, and play her favorite music, things that could keep her connected to us. However, Rob's needs were the opposite, no touching or speaking. It was hard sitting at the bedside at such a distance, but I knew that was what was needed from me at that moment. Even after his recovery, Rob's body would involuntarily jump, especially when touched, and too much stimulus would force him to withdraw to his room.

At the time of Rob's brain surgery, we had just returned home from Arizona, and Mike got our motor home set up in Rob's driveway. Seneca was in middle school, so I registered her for school and drove her to her appointments until Rob started driving again. I loved helping Rob with Seneca, managing all his doctor's calls and paperwork, and cooking for him. After his death, it was only natural I would take care of Seneca's affairs, and having her living with us also helped both of us heal.

Rob loved chicken strips and frozen chicken Cordon Bleu, so I always made extra for him. For his birthday one year, he asked me to make Fiesta Corn Salad, a recipe he had cut out of the newspaper. I didn't think it sounded good, but I made it. It was delicious. You will find this recipe included in the chapter *Treasured Family Recipes*.

2001~Jennifer's lungs were at such a high risk for pneumonia they ordered the rotating bed. A bed that is often used for burn victims and spinal cord injuries. It looks intimidating; hopefully, it will do the job and keep her lungs clear.

With the transfer to the new bed complete, she then laid on a rigid platform with partitions outlining her arms and legs. Locked into place, my little snow angel slowly moved. The delivery person explained the controls and the speed and degree of the rotation. The bed rotated left forty degrees, paused for three minutes, returned to the starting spot, remained there for three minutes, rotated right forty degrees, and remained there for three minutes before returning to the center. After three minutes, the preset program continued. As always, I hated it when visiting hours were over, but now I had a date to put on my calendar, only four days away, December 11. The taxi returned me to the same lonely room, and I escaped into my dreams.

"Good morning, my little rotating snow angel." Each hour that passed brought me closer to her waking up. I wanted my sleeping beauty to magically awaken, and I wanted someone to awaken me from this nightmare. However, fear of the unknown assaulted my thoughts. I focused on the monitor, which was her way of speaking. The nurse increased the pain medication and said that high blood pressure signaled pain. My hatred for the new bed grew: every three minutes, it rotated her away from my grasp.

A friend stopped by that morning, prayed with me, and told me that the guardian angels wouldn't be enough for Jennifer—and that God was at her bedside.

There are different beliefs about angels. The Bible speaks of ministering angels coming to help or guide us. Some believe a relative who has passed can be an angel, but I see no evidence in the Bible to support that thought.

I will never understand the power of God. I can only share my experiences, and I know I may not remember every little detail. Was it cold and rainy that day, or was the sun high in the sky? I know my life adventures are true. While sharing my first book at a writing conference, one editor suggested I write my book as a fiction. She worried readers might have trouble believing it. I wish my life was a fiction novel that I could rewrite the story to suit me. Since God has placed me here at this time, how can I refuse my circumstances? His mysterious ways are not for me to question. Although, I do question if God is closing his door to me right now. Sharing our stories is so important; that is one reason I am sharing Jennifer's story; it is a life story that should be told and retold. We must believe God catches our tears. However, it is up to you to accept or reject God's promises and miracles. If I don't share the good news of Christ, how can I call myself a Christian?

    1977~I recall a stressful time when I experienced an angel sent to deliver a goodbye message from my dying father. Gary and I were sleeping in the front room of a rented apartment one block from the Texas hospital where Dad was battling cancer. Mama and two-year-old Jennifer were sleeping in the back bedroom. Jennifer's hollering "Mommy" awoke me. I jumped out of bed and rushed down the hall. Mama was coming toward me. We quickly realized no one had cried.

    In the quietness of the hall, the color drained from Mama's face; she cried, "I need to get to the hospital." As she opened the front door, my brother, Billy, was on the steps and tearfully said, "Dad's gone." Mama and I knew that the voice we'd heard had been an angel carrying Dad's final goodbye.

    I pray that today, my daughter's angel continues guiding and protecting her.

    19 November 2022~I trust that God sent an army of ministering angels and ushered Rob home. I am thankful God commanded his angels to guard me from the events of that night, and that God still holds those memories.

4

Silent Tears

"Record my misery; list my tears on your scroll. Are they not in your record?"
Psalm 56:8

10 December 2001~Jennifer's bed continued to rock her to the rhythm of the breathing machine.

One day until surgery, and now we wait.

Rob stuck his head in the room. "Logan is in the waiting room." My three-year-old grandson patted his lap and said, "Grandma, lay your head here." I took a rest in the company of my grandson while Rob visited his sister. Their good-bye hugs tugged on my heart.

Immediate family and clergy visited Jen's bedside throughout the day, covering her with healing prayers. The conversation ebbed to a quiet mumble—I wasn't the only one who was afraid. I begged the nurse to let me spend the night. Placing her hand softly on my knee, she said, "Not tonight. You must take care of yourself."

Rob dropped me off at the motel. "Love you, Mom. We'll pick you up in the morning." My savior rocked me in His arms.

On 11 December, 2001~Family stood at the bedside, and the rotating bed stopped. Gathered around Jen, my closest friend prayed for protection for my daughter and guidance for Doctor Barker and his team.

Medical assistants positioned themselves on each side of the bed, slid their hands underneath Jennifer's sleeping body, and quickly transferred her onto the small gurney. I walked along her bedside until the double doors swung open. My quivering lips lingered on her cold cheek. I wiped my tears with the back of my hand and said, "We will see you shortly. I love you." I tucked Woody under her arm. He was the only family member allowed through the stainless doors.

We retreated to the surgical waiting room, and friends joined us in the long wait. My oldest brother, Butch, and Mama waited in Loveland for updates. Butch would support Mama in case Jennifer didn't survive. At 12:10 p.m., we received the first phone call from the nurse. "They harvested her bone, and Doctor Barker will begin the neck surgery," she said. The nurse reassured us that everything was going as planned.

As promised, Doctor Barker's nurse called us hourly with updates. Strangers filled and emptied the waiting room. I wanted a face-to-face update. Silence fell over the group as we waited; finally, at 8:05 p.m., Doctor Barker walked through the door that had hypnotized me for nine hours. Bars and screws had been implanted into my daughter's head. My insides quivered as he showed us the digital photo; one thin remaining ligament was all that prevented paralysis or death. "She has a low-grade fever, but that's to be expected. She will be in recovery for a couple of hours." Words of gratitude circled his ears, and good-bye hugs filled our little space. I called Mama with all the wonderful news so she could share it with our satellite support.

The doctor wanted her head to remain motionless, so he ordered that the rotating bed be removed. Gary, Karen, and I retreated to our spots in the ICU waiting room. Crossword magazines lay open in their laps. Gary's voice pierced the silence. "It's eleven o'clock—why are they taking so long to clean her up?" he said as he headed toward the nurses' station. "I'm going to check." The nurse confirmed that she was doing okay and said that they were waiting on the new bed. It was a little before midnight when the nurse stepped into the waiting room. "You can see her now."

I stroked her warm hand and softly spoke. "Jennifer, it's Mom and Dad. You did great, and we are so proud of you. Keep fighting." How I wanted to cry when I saw more tubes coming from her body. "I've tucked Woody under your arm; he'll stay with you while we get some sleep. Good night, sunshine. I'll see you in the morning." Gary and Karen said their goodbyes to Jennifer, then dropped me off at my motel. Sobbing flooded my pillow, and once I found my escape into the world of nothingness.

2003~I love the creativity my son shared while he walked this earth. I envision him sitting at the lakeside, writing poetry and conversing with Jesus.

Rob wrote the following statement and poem while attending Oral Roberts University. "We must put God back in the classroom and uphold the teachings of Jesus Christ. We must remind children that if they can't find God in a flower or another child, they won't be able to find him in the Bible. In closing, we as educators light that lamp that shines on the path of the child."

<u>Nature (Excerpt)</u>
The topic is nature, one that I will nurture,
One that we will seek, one in which I will give you a peek,
The books I read, of well, they were three,
The Lorax, Biology a study of the Ecosystem and Oh Say Can You Seed,
The two were obvious, written by Doctor Seuss
These were fun written to muse.
The other was boring; all of the information and facts,
All within the pages are nice and densely packed.
Doctor Seuss's books were fun to the point and silly,
learned more of them, no-nonsense, no really.
If for me to teach, I had to pick,
No doubt, to me, without a lick,
I would choose educational books with pictures that are fun
Books that rhyme, have silly words and are full of puns.
I think I know what will work for me,
Books that are fun and to the point
Books that run and tickle the joint
When we read and have fun,
We will have the need

To make the rain disappear and scatter the sun!

12 December 2001~The taxi ran late, causing me to miss morning rounds, but the nurse informed me of her progress and the great news that the respiratory therapist would begin weaning her off the ventilator. Hopefully, her lungs will take over, and she'll be freed from the breathing machine. The day passed slowly; respiratory therapists came and went, each time lowering the breathing machine's work for Jennifer. My eyes were blurry, and I struggled to read aloud, so I ended the chapter and kissed her goodnight. I would always read in the hope that my voice would keep Jennifer connected to this world. More than that, I was reading to shield my heart from Satan's attacks.

"I worry about her mom. I peeked into her heart, and it was overflowing with tears. Her heart's chambers were rumbling with uncontrollable sobbing, and tears were dripping from their walls. Her thoughts were swirling about how I wanted to rock Jenny's mom in my arms."

The following morning, the doctor popped into her room. "Another good night for Jennifer. Today, we're removing the ventilator. The respiratory team and a surgical team will be here in a few hours. If her lungs are too weak, she'll need a tracheotomy—a surgical procedure to create an opening through the neck into the windpipe. The neurologist ordered the sedative lowered so she'll be more alert and able to communicate with you."

Three men in blue scrubs entered the room. A fourth man pushed a cart carrying the sterile, covered surgical equipment. He looked up and said, "Mrs. Kittler, go grab a cup of coffee. We'll be finished when you return."

I heard a faint, raspy whisper. "Mom, what happened? Where am I?" Raising her right arm and touching the metal halo, she said, "What is this?

Mom, I can't move my legs and my arm."

Through my tears, I said, "Oh, sweetheart, you were in a major car accident Thanksgiving weekend. A drunk driver rear-ended you girls while you were stopped at a red light on Thanksgiving weekend." I wondered how much I should tell her. "You injured your neck; the halo is keeping things from shifting."

"But I can't move my legs and my arm. Am I paralyzed?"

"No, you broke your pelvis. You had surgery to repair it." I caught myself before I told her about her strokes; I must wait until she is stronger. I hated all the questions she was firing at me. Will she walk again? Did anyone die?

"Your friends had a few bruises, but they weren't hospitalized. The drunk driver was hospitalized with broken ribs. Jen, you have battled a lot of things these past few days. You are amazing, and you can fight through all the upcoming rehabs. Your dad will be so surprised to hear your voice, even if you do sound like a football player."

My words of encouragement fell short as her crying increased. I know that eventually, the surgery scars will heal, but will self-pity and resentment? I wondered whether she would forgive the drunk driver. Would I?

Barely audibly, she said, "Mom, you said Thanksgiving weekend.

What day is it?"

"Thursday, December thirteenth. You've been in the hospital for twenty-one days." Once again, I explained the surgeries and the reason for the halo. What a wonderful sight, a daughter and her father talking. The decrease of sedatives gave us a brief window of time with her. Each waking moment, Gary and I confirmed our love for her.

November 2022~The days after Rob died are blurry. I was lost, still trying to grasp the truth. And to be honest, I am still trying to grasp the fact we will never share chicken strips or hugs. Thinking back on our last hug. Something was different, the embrace wasn't his usual one-arm hug. Of course, I didn't think anything about it until later. I wonder if Woody could peek into my heart now, would he see me drowning in my silent tears?

Thinking back, Rob said things that didn't make sense until now. None of us know how long the negative thoughts had been attacking him. Satan prowls around like a roaring lion looking for someone to devour, and Rob was a easy prey. He had been weakened by the trials of the brain tumor and worrying about his finances. Satan attacked him on all fronts. He was a young father who loved education and had put his career on hold to be the best single dad. Robert had plans to return to ORU and finish his doctorate. The brain tumor took that dream away and many others. He was beaten down at every turn. Trying to find his normal, he tried working at a coffee shop but couldn't remember the steps to make the specialty coffee, filling orders at a local grocery store, but wasn't fast enough.

The decision to sell the Estes home came quicker than I expected. Originally, we had planned to wait until his youngest graduated, which was two more years. Despite those plans, he decided to rent an apartment in Longmont, saying the place would sell better if his cottage home was empty. The plan after the house sold was that we were both going to find small houses, but he insisted that I get situated first.

A couple of days before he took his life, he had gotten a respiratory infection, and because Covid was still a concern, we hadn't seen each other that week. He had gone to the urgent care, and I asked what they were going to do about it; he answered, "Shoot me, I hope." Where did that come from? My son had never owned a gun and, as far as I knew, never shot one. Rob was a sensitive person, a lover of animals, especially his cats, devoted to his children, and loved writing poetry and art. His actions just didn't match his personality.

2001~With the decrease in Jen's sedatives, every waking moment, her cries filled the room. My words of comfort could not compete with her pain.

"Jennifer, hi. I'm Jane from physical therapy. You've had some rough days, but the doctor would like you to sit up so that we can get your lungs cleared. You can't bear any weight until your pelvis heals. Therefore, my dear, we have a tough challenge. The doctor tells me that you're a fighter." A smile filled Jen's face as Jane continued. "We'll begin slow, and Leon is here to help." With the bed lowered Leon placed his arms under Jennifer's armpits.

"Jen, we're slowly going to swing your legs over the side of the bed. Leon will lift your shoulders, and I'll swing your legs. Tell us if you feel sick or light-headed."

She faintly shouted and then said, "I'm going to fall."

"No, little one. I have a good hold on you, and I won't let you fall," Leon said as he steadied her wobbling back. "You're doing great. Let's try sitting on the edge of the bed for five minutes. We won't let you fall.

Jennifer's face turned grayish-white as she struggled to complete the task asked of her. Simultaneously, Jane gradually swung Jen's legs back onto the bed, and Leon's large hands secured her shoulders. He lowered her head until the halo was resting on the pillow.

Leon fulfilled his promise, "Good job, little one. We'll see you tomorrow."

Tears rushed down her flushed cheeks, and I could sense tears flooding my heart.

After screaming, Jennifer said, "Mom, this halo is heavy, and it hurts. I can't sit on the stupid edge of the bed for five minutes. Why me? Mom, I can't even move my legs without help. What if I can't walk again?"

I took a deep breath and stuffed all my doubts into my heart's black storage chest, marked "Do not open." I managed to say, "I know that right now, this is overwhelming, but you have no choice. Jennifer, you must work through the pain. You will walk again. Remember, it's like eating an elephant—one bite at a time." Caressing her hand in mine, "When you're afraid, remember to call on Jesus; He will be your

39

strength. When your pain is unbearable, Trust me—Jesus will never let you go.

15 December 2001~Jennifer's nights were filled with terrible nightmares. The nurse explained it was ICU psychosis. The glass walls and bright lights had been her home for twenty-two days. You have not experienced normal night-and-day cycles. This will pass.

"Hey, little one, where's that smile? You ready to get out of the bed?"

The giddy Jennifer surfaced. "I'll try. How do I get in if I can't stand up?"

"That's our job, missy. We're going to help you into the wheelchair."

Leon lowered the bed until it was even with the wheelchair. His large hands raised her shoulders while Jane swung her feet over the side of the bed. "You doing okay, missy?" Leon kept his big hands-on Jen's back, preventing her from falling while she caught her breath. She nodded. "Sit here for a few minutes before we transfer you into the chair."

Jane requested another aide, so the three of them whisked her from the edge of the bed to the wheelchair. Leon stood behind Jennifer and placed his hands in the gait belt. He pulled it until her butt touched the back of the chair. "Let's see if you can sit up for ten minutes."

Jennifer's cries filled the room. Leon reclined the wheelchair, taking some pressure off her pelvis. "Here's your little stuffed dog. Since your mom is in the room, we'll be back in ten minutes."

Sweat beads pooled on her pale cheeks. "Mom, please go get them. I can't stand it anymore."

"Only a few more minutes; you've almost made it through five minutes; see if you can make it a little longer."

Tears poured down her face, and she yelled as loudly as her voice would allow, "No! Go get them."

Her body relaxed as the team returned her to bed, and the nurse injected a clear liquid into her IV tube. The nurse praised

Jennifer for making it eight minutes and encouraged her that things would become easier. Since she had tolerated ice chips, they would now try her on thick liquids.

When her dad arrived, she shared how mean I was for not getting the nurse earlier and making her sit in the wheelchair for so long. Hatefully, she said, "I thought I was going to die, and Mom didn't care. Dad, do you think I'll ever walk?"

Thankfully, Gary defended me by reminding her that she needed to do what the therapist told her, and then he even told her not to be so hard on me. "Your mom and I are meeting with the staff at Craig Hospital today; it's one of the best rehabs in the United States. We should have an answer for you, but it's too early. Your pelvis was severely damaged. You need to focus on getting stronger and to do what the therapist tells you."

"But, Dad, it hurts so bad. I don't know if I can do this," her raspy voice screamed.

Gary and I walked down the hall and discussed how and when we should tell Jen the devastating news that she would never drive again. We decided that we needed to wait until she got better. Craig Hospital accepted her, and they gave me a free apartment with a kitchen located across from the hospital.

Rob drove Mama to the hospital to see Jennifer. I was so thankful she took the responsibility off me and relayed all the updates or setbacks to our satellite friends. She would be with me if she didn't have her disabled son to care for. Jennifer and Rob were close to their grandmother. They each had such a special bond with her. On Friday nights, Jennifer and she would share the 'Brown Bag Burger Special.' Whenever Rob was in her neighborhood, he would quickly visit and raid her fridge or bum a cigarette. She always kept a little glass candy dish filled with orange slice candy, especially for them. Included in the chapter *Through My Eyes My Son's Verses* is the poem titled *Grandmother*, written by Robert. It was accepted into the National Library of Poetry. He made it a beautiful wall plaque that hung on my mama's wall up till her death and now hangs on my wall.

The fluttering of Jen's eyes signaled that it was time for goodbyes. Mama kissed her namesake, Jennifer Marie, and then said, "Uncle Butch sends his love. He sends you some books for when you feel better. He'll visit when you're settled into the rehab hospital. Of course, we haven't told Billy about your accident—he just wouldn't understand."

Jennifer said her tearful goodbye to her grandma and expressed her thankfulness to Rob for driving her, "Love you all. Tell Uncle Butch thanks for the books. I can't wait to see him."

I rode home with them to get her some clothes for rehab. Jennifer's depression pained my heart, and I needed a night free of the fight-for-life helicopters whose landing pad was outside her window. One night, I heard doctors rushing, and then a silence filled the halls. I suddenly knew the sound of death.

2022~The challenges Rob faced were not all physical; he struggled with remembering how to do things. Re-learning how to button his shirt was painful to watch. He battled with the blank spaces in his brain as he searched for information he knew should be there. I do not think any of us really understood his struggles. I solely believe that unless you have experienced that gap in your memory/brain, no explanation provides comfort. I was at a loss for what my son was experiencing until now; sadly, it is too late to help him. The quilt stretched out on my sofa reminds me that I lost a part of myself that night when we were summoned to Rob's apartment. I have no memory of the arms that wrapped the patch work quilt around me or being taken to the hospital. That feeling of searching for something that should be within reach but is unreachable is hard to describe, and for myself, I am content not finding that memory.

I sat by Jen's bedside for months and supported her, but now I am not even able to support her during her grief; she is the strong one. How I wish Rob would have cried out. He kept it all inside, didn't share his struggles with his close friends, and didn't confide in his family. Navigating the overwhelming roadblocks became difficult for him, and he couldn't see a way through, then Satan whispered a way out. I wish I could have told him to hold Jesus's hand. Rob accepted Christ in 2000. I wasn't surprised to see Bible verses and the Prayer of Jabez were written throughout his journal. 1 Chronicles 4:10, *"Jabez cried out to the God of Israel, "Oh that you would bless me and enlarge my territory! Let your hand be with me and keep me from harm so that I will be free from pain. And God granted his request."* Healing doesn't always come as we walk this earth. It gives me great comfort knowing my son is resting in the arms of Jesus and is safe from Satan's attacks.

    Fear is from the devil, and it is powerful. After Rob's surgery, he struggled to re-learn the basics of self-care, and I think he believed some things would never return to normal. I know for myself; I fear how I will respond when I finally accept the fact Rob is gone or worse, if those memories of that night surface. Fear is a real thing and sometimes can't be explained away; that is when all I can do is reach out and hold the hand of Jesus. When Jennifer was fearful, it was easier to comfort and encourage them to continue fighting through the rehab. Even when she was vocal and mad at the world, I knew what she was feeling, but Rob was different; he withdrew to himself. Looking back, I realize I never saw the despair that haunted him.

    After Rob's brain surgery, I jumped deeply into the mothering mode. I took care of all his financial and medical paperwork, navigating doctor appointments, and sorting insurance papers while keeping his household needs met. I felt needed. So, I can see why, after his death, I immediately went into bookkeeping mode. I felt needed and didn't have to focus on the truth; he was gone, and I was letting God catch my silent tears and place them in His jar.

5

Gods Plans–Satan's Lies

"For I know the plans I have for you," declares the LORD,
"plans to prosper you and not to harm you, plans to give you hope
and a future."
Jeremiah 29:11

2001~The middle of December welcomed Jennifer with the dream and visions of recovery. Shopping for Jennifer's new wardrobe was more than picking out clothes; it was the beginning of a new journey. Jogging pants, oversized T-shirts and even shoes replaced faded nightgowns. Jennifer would now be dressing for the road to healing and recovery. Everyone worried if she would be able to face her limitations, could I? We are stepping into a world of unknowns that we must walk through.

Over the next few days, Jennifer fought this new world in which she woke up. The halo was awkward and painful. Daily, she pushed through the challenge of sitting in her wheelchair. Through preserving and with Leon's and Jane's encouragement, Jennifer accomplished the goal of sitting in the wheelchair for ten minutes. During the procedure of removing the last drainage tube and chest port, the gatekeeper said, "Her left side is responding quickly to my commands—she is ready to be transferred out of intensive care and go to a hospital that specializes in spinal cord/brain injuries." He placed his hand on my daughter's shoulder," You are a brave lady. Keep working on your recovery."

Her hoarse voice said, "Thank you. Thank you."

I enveloped his warm, extended hand in both of mine and said, "Thank you so much for everything you did for my daughter. It meant a lot when you asked your mom to pray for her." He nodded as he left.

Jennifer's fear of the unknown continued, and she asked her dad the same questions, how much longer would she need to wear the halo? Would she walk again? She fixated on the drunk driver. Gary slowly spoke to her, laying out each detail. As redundant as the facts were to us, she listened as if the answers were falling on her ears for the first time. The lines between her eyes tightened as Gary explained the failed arrest of the driver. When the police tried to arrest him, he denied that he was the man who'd been released from the hospital and showed them a different driver's license.

Her fearful response was always, "It isn't fair."

Her dad always replied, "Yes, it may not be fair; however, you can't focus on him. You must concentrate on getting better. You must push yourself."

Everyone was anxious and nervous about the news that Jennifer was transferring to a rehab center. The decision was left up to the doctors what place would meet her many needs. The receiving hospital reviewed her chart and agreed to accept her, as every patient isn't accepted. Gary and I were excited that Craig Hospital had accepted her. We heard wonderful success stories, and it is a neurorehabilitation and research hospital located in Englewood, Colorado.

2018~Rob, going to a rehab facility seemed to be a step backward in his mind. I didn't take into consideration that Rob and Jennifer have such different personalities. Rob loved his seclusion and his simple life. Being a single dad, he had children to worry about. Jennifer enjoyed being with people. In their careers, Rob was a self-starter; his love for new adventures took him on many paths—owner of his own real estate company, Lincoln Logs, named after his son, Logan, children's bookstore manager/owner, elementary school teacher and ghost tour guide for the popular Stanley hotel.

Rob's creativity led to the publication of his first book, *Can't Sleep, Count Sheep*. A few of his poems are included in the chapter, *Through My Eyes My Son's Verses*. I cherish a recording of Rob reading from his book for the Longmont literacy reading program. He had such a neat way to make his poems dance. My favorite reading is. *Bees In The Trees*.

Jennifer didn't like change; she was content with remaining in the same field of work and working her way up from a simple clerk to a human resource specialist. 2024 will mark Jennifer's twenty-eight-year anniversary, with many recognitions hanging on her wall or sitting on her desk. Her dad would be so proud to hear about her promotion and her new department.

Rob loved helping people, and my heart was warmed when his friends contacted me after his funeral, sharing their stories of how he had helped them find a house or helped a single mom move. That is who Rob was; he gave and gave of himself and was respectful of me. Agreeing to go to a rehab facility was out of respect and his love for me. I truly wish I had foreseen how it would crush his spirits.

Both of my children were fighters, so it didn't surprise me Rob improved with home therapy. Yet, it wasn't the physical challenges that he battled; it was processing information and remembering small details. I purchased a large print calendar and helped him organize his appointments. He made his to-do list daily and worked on it. I love to-do lists, but Rob's list recorded the simple routine, mundane things we do without thinking. Clutter and several people talking at once stressed him and caused his brain to shut down, forcing him to withdraw to his darkened room. Lights bothered him. He often complained that he felt a light was on in his head. After months of therapy, he did begin driving again; he never regained his balance completely, so he sold his bike. Inside his journal, he taped a saying, 'I am tired of explaining myself to people who only see things from their perspective.'

2001~ The ambulance transported Jennifer to her new home; no one knew how long she would be there, as the work was up to

Jennifer. Gary and I were surprised they had placed her on the brain injury floor instead of the spinal floor. The nurse explained it was because of her previous strokes. After getting Jennifer settled into her new bed and introducing her to her care team, the nurse told Jennifer, "Next week, you'll have a work schedule but nothing on the weekends. The doctor expects you to attend and participate in each class."

"I can't even lift my legs. How can I do anything?"

The nurse reassured her a talented team would support her daily. We knew Jennifer would be pushed to her limits every day so she would become strong and independent again. At this point, we didn't know the damage from the strokes. The orthopedic surgeon couldn't guarantee Jennifer would be able to walk again without assistance. I knew I would be pushed to help her while keeping myself positive. I was so thankful for the tiny apartment; a percolator and microwave made life a little simpler for me, but the best part was I didn't have to depend on the taxi; I could walk to her room through a secure walkway.

Jennifer had been in the ICU for over a month and only received the basic bed baths, so we decided to shave her legs. Unable to raise her legs, we did the best we could while she was lying flat. I could hear the fear in her voice as Jen's questions surfaced once again. "Will I ever be able to lift my legs? Turn over? Will I walk again? Why did this happen?"

"Hush, Jen, you're talking too fast. Slow down—we'll take it one day at a time. I understand that this is hard for you. One moment, you're enjoying Thanksgiving, and then you wake up with tubes coming out of your nose, and you're caged in the halo. It's a lot to process. But you're in the best hospital in the United States; people worldwide come here. We are so blessed that the hospital accepted you. Let's focus on recovery. Leave the 'whys' in God's hands. Right now, we're going to finish those legs." Do I tell her that complete recovery might look different than before? I don't have the heart to tell her that the stroke prevents her from processing new information and that she repeatedly asks the same things.

"Thanks, Mom, you're right. I don't know what I would do without you." What day is it?

"Saturday, December twenty-second. Three days till Christmas. Jen, you'll have lots of visitors this weekend. Rob will be here soon, so I'm riding back home with him. I'll return early on Monday so that I can help you dress. No more nightgowns—plus, the physical therapist wants you to wear walking shoes."

"Shoes—that's stupid. I can't even lift my legs, much less stand. Do you think this halo will freak out, my friends?"

"No way. Everyone is so excited to finally see you." I was glad Doctor Pena dropped in for morning rounds and interrupted her train of conversation. However, her first question to the doctor was whether she would ever walk again.

"It's too early to tell since it was an open-book break. Imagine butterfly wings." He arranged his hands with his fingertips touching. "See its body as a ring." He quickly spread his fingers apart, keeping only his pinky fingers touching. "That is what happened to you. Based on the X-rays, it looks like you have a metal plate and multiple screws on your pubic bone. It looks like you have large screws on both sides, fixating the left and right sacroiliac joints. The surgeon did an excellent job of giving you your wings back."

Jennifer constantly nodded as she listened. The look on her face said, "Oh, really? I didn't know I broke my pelvis." She finally spoke. "Thank you for explaining all of that."

"Let me look at your stomach. The nurse said you've complained of it hurting." After a few pushes below her belly button, he said, "I'm ordering an ultrasound of your liver and gallbladder. A tunnel connects Craig Hospital and Swedish Medical Center. You'll travel through it many times; all the testing is performed there. Our spine surgeon will come by later and look at your neck incision."

Rob opened the door, and Logan bounced into the room with a huge smile. Doctor Pena said, "Looks like you have company; I'll stop in tomorrow morning."

While she visited with Rob, I busied myself with unpacking the rest of Jen's porcelain angels and displaying all the lovely get-well/birthday cards on the white wooden bookcase. Laughter filled her room; I welcomed the change.

Jennifer loved cats also and still had her cat from third grade, Slippers. However, she did fudge the truth about finding him abandoned by the riverbed. She actually paid five dollars at the pet store in our neighborhood. Rob and Logan would go by her apartment and check on him. Logan made her smile while he told stories about all his hiding places and finally discovering him under the kitchen sink. But when Jennifer began to slur her words, everyone knew her brain had enough visiting for her today, and it was time to leave.

Logan blew her a kiss. Being careful not to hurt her, I gently kissed her cheek and said, "Call me at bedtime, and I'll see you on Monday morning."

"Where are you going?"

"I'm sorry, I thought I mentioned that I'm riding back home with Rob for the weekend." The puzzled look on her face reminded me once again of her brain injury.

The smile vanished from her face. "I wish you wouldn't go, but I know you have things that you need to do." I gave her Woody and reminded her to call me at bedtime.

2022~Rob kept all his fears to himself. Occasionally, he would comment on how he wanted to feel normal, but I never understood what he meant until it was too late. I wish he would have cried out to me; I would have found a way to rescue him from the grip Satan had on him. I don't know much about mental illness, but I believe the voices they hear drown out all others.

Jennifer cried and screamed her fears; I always felt I could reason with her and calm those inner storms. Woody, as silly as it may seem, really helped.

I thought Rob meant normal, as he wanted to be able to process things as quickly as before and return to work. I know it scared him when he couldn't think as before; he knew something was different. But no one knew how much the brain surgery damaged his cerebellum. The old Rob never returned. An example of how his brain now worked was when giving me his grocery list; He would say, pick me up the red rice in the white box. I thought when he said he just wanted to be normal again, he meant to process things; I never knew he had dark thoughts he battled. Now I realize he was crying out for help even back then. I had no idea his struggles ran so deep. His darkness was stronger than any of us saw. He had so much to live for. I don't believe he wanted to die, but he wanted the pain and confusion to end.

We are stepping into a world of unknowns we must walk through.

Weeks after his service, I requested Rob's medical records; he had gone to urgent care a couple of days before with a respiratory infection. I was searching for an answer to why he did it, hoping the doctor had given him bad news about another tumor or something. God used my pain that day as I picked up his records. I had to give the clerk his death certificate to make a copy. When she returned, she commented, "I know you want to know the reason, but I deal with that thought every day, and seeing your pain today has given me a reason to fight another day. This young lady wore the same mask as my son did, happy and smiling on the outside but struggling on the inside. We hugged and cried together. Later, I went back and gave her a candle and my phone number. She has never reached out, but I pray she finds a reason each day to choose life.

I genuinely believe when a Christian loses their way, overcome with despair and darkness that influences them into taking their own life, they are still greeted into heaven with open arms by Jesus. His mercy and grace are never-ending. Satan whispers lies to me and wants to use that night to gain a foothold in my heart. But I will not allow it. I choose to see the image of God sending his band of angels to carry Rob to his heavenly home.

Gary, Rob's dad, died at the age of 75 from Covid in January 2022. I have a text from Rob right after that saying, "Mom, please don't leave me; what would I do without you?" I am so thankful I've kept so many of his texts and emails; texting was the main way we communicated. I re-read them often. Rob was always so appreciative and would tell me so or write a little note on a scrap of paper, all of which I still have stuck in my Bible. But now I am faced with figuring out my world without him.

This note holds a special place in my heart. It was 1994, and Rob had graduated from high school and would be venturing out on his own. He gave me a book on flower arrangements for my birthday, and this is what was written inside. "Here's a book to keep you entertained because I won't be around; arrange your flowers and thoughts, but never disarrange your feelings about loving me. Thanks for everything you have ever done. love Rob"

2024~As I pick fresh flowers from my garden and refresh your cemetery bouquet, please know I will never disarrange my feeling of loving you.

I ask myself daily, how can I survive without you? I will hold onto the promise God has a plan for me to prosper and give me hope for my future, knowing I will see you again. He will protect me from the lies Satan throws at me.

6
Terrified

"God is our refuge and strength, an ever-present help in trouble. Therefore, we will not fear, though the earth gives way, and the mountains fall into the heart of the sea, though its waters roar and foam and the mountains quake with their surging. "
Psalms 46:1-3

23 December 2001~The respite refreshed my weary soul. I tried to focus on buying a Christmas present for my grandson, but flashes of my broken daughter struggling to move her legs overshadowed what little joy I found. Christmas shopping completed phone calls, and mundane chores stole the rest of my day. A quick glance at my watch and a sigh of my heart said that I would have to wait hours for Jennifer's bedtime call.

My heart jumped as the phone rang, the caller ID glowed Craig Hospital. Thinking it was too early for Jen's bedtime call. When I answered, I could barely hear Jennifer speaking, "Jennifer, what is going on? Who is yelling? Jennifer, talk to me," I screamed.

"Mrs. Kittler, this is nurse Carol. The nurses are rushing Jennifer to Swedish Hospital's emergency room; she is throwing up blood." The high pitch of her voice made it clear that it was serious.

The long ride to the hospital was grueling. I could not get a handle on my thoughts. Why had I left her? I should have stayed. The video replayed in my head, highlighting the pain in her eyes when they tightened the four screws through her skin into the bone of her forehead. The vision of her broken body jumping and twitching filled my mind's eye. My brain was screaming and would not shut off the images. Why? Enough is enough; I do not think I can be strong anymore. The star-filled sky reminded me that I was not alone. I prayed that the Creator who placed each star in the heavens would provide me with the strength I needed. I had to trust Him and not let fear dominate my thoughts.

The Swedish Hospital emergency-desk attendant escorted me to the intensive care unit.

"Mrs. Kittler, glad you are here. See if you can calm her down. The sedation is not working. She is fighting and pulling her IV tubes."

The fast-talking nurse scared me; she looked as if she had bad news. Her voice quivered as she explained that Jen had a bleeding ulcer, and the doctor cauterized it, but she had lost a lot of blood, and I had to be prepared for how pale Jennifer looked and was very hysterical.

"Is she in any danger now?"

"Yes, this is serious; she is on the critical list. There is a problem matching her blood; she has had so many units that her body has made antibodies. I am waiting for the lab so we can get the transfusions started." She paused. "Also, she's back on the ventilator, and she is fighting it; see if you can calm her."

"Jen, honey, it is Mom. Listen to me; You must calm down." I squeezed my fingers in between the halo and stroked her hair from her pale face. "You had a bleeding ulcer, but the doctor fixed it; you lost a lot of blood." I forced back the tears and continued. "Calm down, and then they can untie you." I covered her pale hand with mine. "Jennifer, you must focus. Remember, hold Jesus's hand. He will not let you go." I visualized Jesus's hands enveloping both of ours. The storm inside me calmed, but she fought the restraints. The lab tech entered the room with the much-needed plasma. The nurse quickly placed the bag on the IV pole and guided the tubing around the spindles. As the yellowish liquid slowly flowed into my ghostly daughter, I encouraged my frightened daughter to stop fighting the breathing machine, and I also calmed myself enough to hear the latest update from the trauma doctor.

The trauma surgeon explained, "Your daughter was incredibly lucky tonight; she lost lots of blood—they got her here just in time. The plasma will stabilize her until they can get the blood matched. This young lady must have a guardian angel watching over her. The lining of the top part of her lung collapsed, but I was able to repair it. We will need to watch that area. Since she lost so much blood so rapidly, we did not want her brain to be deprived of oxygen. I have ordered a chest X-ray to check her lungs."

The room stood still as Jennifer fought for her life, and for a time, the only sound was the pulsating of the breathing machine. At midnight, my daughter was given the much-needed matching blood. Bag after bag dripped into Jennifer's white body.

I kissed her light-pink cheeks and whispered, "Good night, sweetheart," I needed to get a few hours of sleep before the morning rounds

24 December 2001~ "Good morning, my little sunshine. You look so rosy. You gave us a scare last night. Do not try talking; they put you back on the ventilator." My voice filled the room as I talked nonstop, explaining everything. "You are on your tenth unit and should be full soon. Guess we know why your stomach hurts. Rest now. I talked to your dad. He will be here within the hour." I hated the noise of the breathing machine. The gut-wrenching sound that the respiratory machine made as it suctioned her made me sick to my stomach. I was thankful that the respirator supplied her brain with oxygen. Thinking back about Billy, I knew the consequences when the brain is deprived of oxygen. Brain cells can start dying within five minutes of oxygen loss, and that is what happened to Billy; parts of his brain died.

I could see Gary coming down the hall through the glass ICU doors, and I quickly joined him. "I am so glad you are here; let us talk before you go in. We almost lost her. she lost a lot of blood, and her hemoglobin number dropped to six point nine and at six, she could have died. The top part of her lung collapsed, but he believes that he repaired it. The doctor ordered a chest X-ray to see if there was any damage." My heart was racing; I was talking so fast, explaining everything. I was thankful Gary sat with her while I went and rested.

Gary said, "She is on the eleventh unit of blood, but I thought the body could hold only ten units. The lung specialist came in while you were gone; the x-ray didn't show any damage, and if she continues to improve, they'll remove the ventilator tomorrow."

I was thankful to hear the good news; Gary kissed her goodbye and reassured her that he would return in the morning to celebrate Christmas. I took my place at the bedside and read more of Charlotte's Web to her until I could no longer focus on the pages. I reminded her that tomorrow was Christmas, and everyone would be coming to celebrate with her.

Since she was still on the ventilator, she scribbled on her pad, "I want to spend Christmas in my own room."

"Honey, I know, but you must try to sleep. Pain medication should help. I will be back early in the morning so that I can talk with the doctor."

"Night, Mom." She scribbled.

I slipped on my pajamas and crawled into bed. My cell phone's ringing halted my prayers. The glowing radio displayed that it was 11:50 p.m. I did not want to answer the phone, but I knew that I had to. I feared that Jennifer had taken a turn for the worse. "Mama, what is the matter? Why are you calling so late?"

Running her words together, it is Butch. They rushed him to the emergency room. His heart stopped, and the paramedics did CPR. I am heading there now; I will call you when I know more."

The tightness in my heart kept my tears in check, and I managed to say, "Keep me updated. Love you, Mama."

At that time, my prayers weren't silent. "Are you there? Is this a sick joke that you are doing to our family?" I propped my shaking body against the headboard and struggled to process the news. Tears flooded my room. Was it a dream, or had my one and only safe place been invaded? As I slipped farther into my blanket cocoon, darkness covered me. I once again cried my angry words to Jesus.

Surprised I slept, but the morning alarm reminded me I have a lot to be grateful for, and I felt bad I got so mad at God. Quietly, I prayed, Father, I am sorry; I have a lot to be thankful for. The doctors have told me many times that it is a miracle that Jennifer is alive. I know that it is a miracle that she survived—I know the miracle is from You.

2024~I survived the daily trials of Jennifer's accident and the death of my brother by holding onto Jesus, which is the only thing I can credit to surviving that pain. At that moment, I saw the pain as unbearable, and nothing could be worse than what I was experiencing. I couldn't see the future. Now, I find myself living with this unspeakable pain. Wondering where God was, I realized he was the one holding me up.

Thinking back on how terrified Jennifer was and how hard she fought her restraints to free herself reminded me of my little tike Robs adventure with a straight jacket. It was 1979, and Gary and I had returned from Texas after making funeral arrangements for my grandmother. Mama and her sister stayed with the kids. Rob, wearing his little yellow PJs, ran into the living room carrying Mama's open bottle of heart medication. We couldn't tell if he had swallowed any, so we took him to the emergency room. Not knowing if he had taken any, the doctor ordered this yucky stuff for him to drink so he would throw up. But making a terrified eighteen-month toddler drink yucky stuff was impossible. So, the doctor tried putting him in a little medical straight jacket; Rob fought the restraints and won his freedom. It was a terrible night, holding him, trying to comfort him while they put this tube down his throat, forcing him to throw up. We laugh about it now and credit that night to his love for escape artist tricks and his fear of doctors. He loved watching magic and performing tricks. He often performed his array of magic tricks at children's birthday parties. Rob owned an escape artist straight jacket; when he was no longer performing tricks, it hung in his man cave.

Another cute story, the yellow pajamas were his favorite. When they became too small, he had me cut out the feet. Those cute PJs and Jennifer's little pink dress are displayed in a shadow box on my shelf; the memories warm my heart.

Since his death, I have asked myself a thousand times, what if we had not moved from Estes or what if we had bought Rob's home first and then got us settled somewhere? My world is full of what-ifs, replaying things he said or texted to me and wondering if I should have seen something. But I know this questioning isn't from God. It is from Satan. I constantly tell myself God is with me and will carry me through, but sometimes my weakness wins over. The wave of grief is more like a tsunami rushing over me.

2001~The buzzing alarm woke me from a restless sleep. I pushed my legs from under the covers and placed my feet firmly on the floor. I forced my mind to accept the fact that my oldest brother was in the emergency room. I couldn't be with my mama; my place was with my daughter.

25 December 2001~The ventilator hoses had been disconnected, and Jen's raspy screams filled the void. "Mom, I can't stand this pain. I hate it here. Take me back to my room," she demanded.

Rushing to the nurse's station, "What happened? I've never seen her in this much pain." Her apology for another emergency was hard to accept for missing Jens' scheduled medication. I remembered the urgency that had painted the trauma unit with my daughters' torn clothes and empty bags of blood strewn everywhere; I would want that same urgency for the trauma that pulled the nurses away. Caressing Jen's fist, "The nurse is on her way. Here's Woody. You knocked him to the floor."

The nurse injected a clear liquid into the IV line and softly spoke, "Jennifer, I'm sorry I was late with your morning meds."

Jennifer's only response was a pleading to go back to Craig. However, since she was still running a temperature, the doctor wanted to monitor her for one more day. So thankful the pain medication kicked in before Rob and his family arrived. "Logan, that package looks bigger than you."

"Yep, it's for Aunt Jenny. Merry Christmas."

"Sorry I didn't get you guys anything," she faintlywhispered.

"Jen, don't say you're sorry; you're alive; my big sis is our present."

Logan tugged on the curly, colorful ribbon. Jen's left hand struggled to hold the package steady while her right hand tore the paper. "Thank you, guys, for my candle. It's beautiful. I'm so sorry that you're spending Christmas day at the hospital."

In unison, we said, "Jennifer, stop saying you're sorry." After a short visit, Logan reached through the bed rails, and his little fingers caressed his aunt Jenny's hand.

"I need to call Mama, and then we'll head over to my little apartment and open packages. The hospital cafeteria closes at one o'clock today, so you all go ahead to the cafeteria, and I'll catch up with you."

My heart raced as I completed the phone number. "Mama, how is Butch?"

"Bobbie," silence, then I heard her swallow. "Your brother isn't expected to make it." Another pause, "His doctor wants to meet with the family. Can you come home tomorrow?"

Fighting back the tears, "This is a hard Christmas for us. Love you, and I'll see you tomorrow."

I wiped the tears from my eyes and joined the family. Tuning out Logan's gibberish and picking on my grilled cheese sandwich. "Grandma, hurry. Let's go open presents." Logan's laughter and excitement summoned me back. His joy bounced off the walls as he opened the little cars and the racetrack that Mama had wrapped for me. I watched as he raced the little cars through the empty boxes. I didn't want the time to end; I could feel the ropes around my heart loosening. However, my watch said that it was time to return to the hospital.

My heart tightened as I once again told another lie. I caressed her hand and said, "Jen, Rob is giving me a ride home; I want to celebrate Christmas with Mama and Billy. I'll be back tomorrow afternoon." Her blank look penetrated my hurting heart. Rob and Melissa said their good-byes, and Logan raced his cars once more on his make-believe roadway on Jen's knee and said, "Bye, Aunt Jenny."

26 December 2001~Embracing Butch's wife, Deb, Mama, and I stood at the bedside of my dying brother; the doctor broke the silence. "Let's visit in the conference room." The formal greetings were exchanged, and the drink offers were refused. "Mack's brain was deprived of oxygen for too long. These are not easy decisions. We could insert a feeding tube, transfer Mack to a nursing home, and leave him on the ventilator. I don't think he'll ever regain consciousness. The second choice is to remove life support and to say your good-byes. I would suggest that if you choose that option, you wait until after the first of the year. Death is hard, but death during the holiday season is tougher. Think of Mack when you make the decision. I listened while Deb and Mama asked questions; my numbness prevented me from taking part. So thankful that the decision didn't fall to me. The doctor left the three of us frozen in place. Deb's tearful words finally broke the ice. "We must think of Mack. He would never choose the nursing home and life support. I will have him taken off life support after the holidays like the doctor suggested."

Mama and I remembered that terrible moment when Billy's life support was removed. A memorial had been planned by his friends, but Billy surprised everyone and started breathing on his own. Since Billy was only 40 and still in a coma, they had to put him on the feeding tube and transfer him to a nursing facility. He remained in a coma for almost six months, and after a year in a nursing facility, my mother requested guardianship and moved him to Longmont so she could care for him. Billy never returned to a nursing home after that point.

We assured Deb of our support; her long hug confirmed that she understood I needed to return to my daughter.

27 Decembe2001~I met with Jennifer's psychiatrist before returning to her room and shared the details of my brother's impending death, "Should I tell Jennifer about her uncle Butch? I need direction."

He raised his eyes from her chart. "No, Jennifer is too fragile. I wouldn't share it with any staff, either. I'll schedule extra visits with her when the Swedish Medical Center releases her. A firm handshake ended our visit. With each step toward her room, I pushed the thought of my dying brother into my heart's chamber. That day, my heart split, and I embarked on an unknown path, traveling between two worlds: recovery and death.

Both my children struggled with pain; when they didn't receive their needed medication, the side effects they suffered were terrible. Jennifer's pain was obvious. The trauma of her injuries was never questioned, and increasing her medication was acceptable and condemned when not provided. However, discounting Rob's pain and concerns was very frustrating and hard on Rob. I saw he was treated differently, often condemned, and treated as a drug addict. At times, I was questioned by friends and one doctor who became known as the 'lemon doctor' whether the medication was necessary or was making up the pain. He didn't believe Rob should still be suffering from back and neck pain caused by a previous back injury and neck fusion, and of course, complaining about light in your brain wasn't logical. He suggested that Rob cut out all lemons from his diet so that he would feel better. Of course, we did find a new GP that helped Rob with pain management. The lemon joke was something Rob and I laughed about, often even including a lemon in our gifts to each other. That was Rob making lemonade out of lemons. After Rob's death, Emma had asked for a lemon cake for her 21st birthday. I found the most delicious recipe and tweaked it a little; that lemon cake recipe has become a new family favorite.

Here's another event I witnessed. Rob was having a severe headache, and his neurologist in Estes Park didn't like the look of his incision. After reviewing his latest MRI, she urged Rob to go to the emergency room, where he had the surgery. I drove my son to the ER, hoping he would find relief, but our hopes were met with disappointment and humiliation. The surgeon's partner was the on-call doctor. After a brief look at my son's incision, he replied, "I've seen worse," then he added, "Neurologists an neurosurgeons don't always agree; your MRI is fine," then sent my son home.

  I believe from the beginning, if Rob's pain management had been approached as a tool to control anxiety and chronic pain, just maybe he wouldn't have been so hard on himself and accepted his need for medication instead of feeling condemned.

  Drug addiction is a huge problem in our country, and I don't completely understand it all, but I do know people do get lost in searching for that balance of pain control, and I know Rob struggled to find that balance. So, did dependency on pain relief turn into addiction? I don't know, but I have seen what happens when someone's pain isn't managed.

  Rob loved Christmas; we could always tell the packages he wrapped; the best way to describe his wrapping was more like a tuck-and-fold approach. As a child, Christmas bows and boxes were his favorite; more than the surprise was hiding inside. I remember one year when Rob was a toddler; his dad wrapped up a huge box full of boxes and bows. Rob played for hours, creating villages of boxes.

  Rob died in November, and he had already bought my Christmas present—A Grandma brag board for pictures. I don't believe his action that morning was a planned event; he just fell into a low spot, terrified of the future. And couldn't navigate his way out. I was oblivious to anything going on with him that day and didn't pray for him. I texted him that morning about a cold he had and suggested Mucinex. My last text didn't even say we loved each other. I always texted that, and he would respond with "ditto" or a heart emoji. Regret is one reason I have placed the small ring dish he gave me in my china cabinet, so it doesn't' break. I will always cherish the simple words written on the dish, 'Remember I love you, Mom.'

Prayer is an odd thing; I have prayed for successful surgeries for both my children. I have also prayed that that God would rescue family members dying from cancer and covid and end their suffering. I feel like when my son needed my prayers the most, he was alone, and as a mother, I was cheated from walking with him during his dark moments. Accepting God's way is hard, and I find myself confused. Then I recall what Elizabeth Elliot said about prayer, "To Pray, 'Thy will be done,' I must be willing if the answer requires it that my will be undone."

All I can do is throw myself into God's arms. During my weak moments, my mind wonders what Rob was thinking the moment he decided to end it. I race to God, find my refuge within His arms and find strength to face another day.

7

Split Worlds

"May the God of hope fill you with all joy and peace as you trust in him, so that you may overflow with hope by the power of the Holy Spirit."
Romans 15:13

2001~As I returned to the recovery world, "Why did you stay gone for so long? I hate it here. Now the doctor says I must stay here for one more night—not sure why."

Before I could answer, the door slid open. "Hey, girl. It's Lois from Craig."

"Lois, I miss you all so much. I hate it here. Sorry for throwing up blood everywhere."

"Oh, Jen, that comes with the job. Kurt says hi. Gotta get back; I just wanted to sneak over and say hello. I heard you're coming back tomorrow—yay!"

I placed Woody on her tummy and tucked the covers under her chin. "Hopefully, tomorrow, we can return to your room. It doesn't seem so hospitable. Is that even a word?" She tried to laugh.

Three days after Christmas, giggles filled the tunnel as the aides from Craig whisked the transport gurney around the curves. Lois got Jennifer situated and did a body check for skin breakdown. "Sweets, those young nurses over there better have rotated you every two hours. You didn't have any breakdown when you left here, and you'd best not have any now." Nurses constantly popped into her room, saying, 'Welcome home.'

Kurt promised he wouldn't let her pain get unmanageable, and within minutes, her furrowed brow relaxed, and her tightened muscles followed.

"Jennifer, we have so much to be grateful for. I know the past week has been tough, but now we concentrate on healing and your future." But I didn't want to look into my future; the removal of my brother's life support and saying my final goodbye weighed heavy on my heart.

"Mom, I know I should be thankful, but some days are harder than others."

"I know it's hard, but we take one day at a time, and some days we take one minute at a time." I tucked Woody under the covers and kissed them good night.

The mustiness of my apartment hit me in the face; I was learning to befriend the silence and emptiness. After a quick shower, I burrowed under the thick quilt. I knew that sleep was my only escape. The quiet was filled with memories of my brother and questions about why all of this happened. Then a voice—not an audible voice—*Why are you so mad at Me? Do as you tell your daughter to do. Hold My hand.* I dangled my hand out from underneath the cover, a peacefulness filled my heart.

The morning welcomed the same routine and the repeated worries that my daughter voiced, "Mom, do you think these thoughts of wanting to die will ever go away? The doctor dropped in and prescribed a stronger depression medication to help me."

"You know that we've talked about this since you were sixteen. Depression is a chemical imbalance in the brain. Now, with the trauma of the accident, I can see why he increased your medication. Medication is a tool that God has given doctors, but you must do your part and stop the negative inner chatter quickly. Don't let Satan get a foothold."

"I'll try, but I can't believe I lost a month of my life; when do you think I'll leave this place? How will I get into my apartment? I can't climb stairs. Mom, what if I never walk again?"

"Jennifer Marie, slow down. You're chattering like a chipmunk. Craig is a wonderful hospital—they work miracles here. Never forget that nothing is impossible for God."

Tears pooled in her eyes as she whispered, "Thank you, Mom. The unknown scares me."

Within minutes of taking her morning medication, a soft whistling sound emerged from my sleeping beauty. I tucked the white woven blanket under her chin, covering the cold metal harness. Medication helped her escape the intense pain, but mine surfaced as I had to face the loss of my oldest brother.

I quickly found a secluded place on the patio and took a deep breath as I called my mother. Her soft-spoken words warmed my cold heart, "Are you doing, okay?"

"They have Jennifer's pain under control. She's better."

"No, I meant, how are you doing?"

"It's hard. I can't talk to anyone about Butch; I feel so fake walking around with a smile on my face while my heart is breaking. I feel like I am dishonoring Butch; I can't even talk about him. Plus, I keep lying to Jennifer; I don't have the heart to tell her that her dad cleaned out her apartment and all her belongings are boxed up and stored in his basement. It's hard. Rehab classes start on Monday, and I'm sure that she'll have lots of visitors this weekend. I'll have Rob pick me up and come home tonight. I love you."

"Love you too and tell Jennifer that I send my love." I was glad that Mama's sister would be there for her, as I didn't have the energy to be a daughter.

Jennifer and I spent the rest of the day in a world of nothingness. After her afternoon nap, I told her that Rob would come for a visit and ride home with him for the weekend.

"But, Mom, you were just there. You weren't here when I got sick. Please don't go."

A weight pressed on my chest. "Honey, I must finish Billy's year-end analysis for the court; you know it can't be late. I'll be back early Monday morning, and you'll have lots of visitors over the weekend."

Rob stayed through Jen's dinner hour—if you can call it a protein shake dinner. Kissing her goodbye and reminding her of my bedtime call, I quickly left, so my tears stayed dammed. We headed home in silence.

Darkness and emptiness covered me that morning—negative jabber invaded my head; he's the oldest; he's responsible for our aging mom and our disabled brother. I'm the baby of the family—he can't leave me. I wanted to hibernate, but the pull to see my brother won out; Mama and I joined Deb at the bedside of my dying brother. I spoke loudly as I read from his Bible so that my voice would overshadow his rhythmic breathing machine. After saying her goodbyes, Mama and her sister returned home. Deb and I stayed at his bedside for the rest of the day. There was an ache in my heart, knowing that on January 3, they would remove his life support.

After Jennifer's bedtime call, I camouflaged myself with a thick blanket and cried my prayers.

2022~When a traumatic event erupts in our world, scrambling the puzzle pieces, it is hard to fit life pieces into the puzzle as before, and that is okay. When Jennifer was in the hospital, and my brother died, I was not able to be a daughter to my hurting mama. Now I find it difficult being a wife to Mike, a mother to Jennifer, and a grandmother to Rob's children. Our lives are also changed but not ruined.

Rob enjoyed motivational speakers. I can't recall the speaker's name, but Rob invited me to go with him to listen to a motivational speaker in Denver. Whenever I went out to his house, a book on tape would play, or he would listen to music. Rob and I both enjoyed a lot of the same books; one of my favorites is *The Practice of Brother Lawerence*, a book I gave Rob and saw still in his collection. However, the sharing of books ended when our lives became busy.

The unknown can be a paralyzing and dark place to venture into. Our minds fill the gaps with all the what if's we can imagine. Eventually, the dark thoughts win over, freezing our progress. All of us were concerned about how the brain tumor was changing his world. But no one ever thought that he wouldn't accept the changes and take his own life.

I can't recall a time Rob suffered from anxiety attacks or was afraid of venturing out into the world. By his senior year, he had read *Walden Pond* by Henry David Thoreau; that book shaped his world. Graduating early, Rob packed his little Honda and went on a road trip to Massachusetts. He loved the peacefulness of Walden Pond. As a member of the Thoreau society, Rob would often visit Massachusetts.

<u>Sincere Lord Sincere</u>
As I draw closer to my dreams
Or is reality really what it seems
I see the lake, the stars, the sun and even the moon
I know it ends, and all of it is over to soon
But I shall start today, now and here
To live my life simplistic, simply,
Simplicity is so real and so dear to who I pray
Sincere Lord Sincere

When he came home for his first visit, he focused on simplifying his life; he would say, if it collects dust, it must go, so he cleaned his room and threw away stuff. However, Rob rotated in and out of that mind set. He would go through phases of getting rid of things; then, he would buy a big-screen TV later. A lot of his purchases were for his kids. One summer, he ordered a foam pit for the spare room. His house was always filled with kids jumping into the blue foam boxes. He made life fun for them; he turned the simple game of hide and seek into a chase adventure. When Logan and Emma were toddlers, they lived in the downstairs apartment. They would wait until they heard their dad's car pull into the driveway, and then they would hide in their special hiding spots. Rob would search and pretend to be a claw and would chase them throughout the house.

Seneca told me about another game he played with them, hot and cold. Jennifer and Rob often played this game as children when searching for a hidden object. But Rob put his own spin on the game, making it more adventurous. He hid money throughout the house, in books and even in wall sockets.

As an adult, Rob had two special places in which he found solace. His first love, of course, was Walden Pond in Massachusetts. It warms my heart that Emma and Seneca returned a little part of him to Walden Pond. They commented that they could see why their dad was drawn to the peacefulness of the nature trails and lake.

Another place Rob retreated was the Prayer Tower situated on the Oral Roberts University campus, designed for the purpose that communication with God must always be the focus of life. I recall one time when he was upset; he called me and told me he was taking a road trip to the Prayer Tower. I don't know how often he took that road trip. Jennifer and I visited the 200-foot glass and steel tower when he graduated from ORU.

I believe Rob's love for nature fueled him to push through the physical challenges so he could return to the outdoors. A couple of years after his brain surgery, he returned to short hikes, but he never made it to the top of Longs Peak in Rocky Mountain National Park, a 14er, with his son, which was their dream to do together. However, Logan and Krystin fulfilled Rob's unattainable dream and rested him high on the Colorado mountaintop.

Rob often overdid his simplifying life too far. At his funeral, his best friend shared that Rob only had two forks and two spoons, with Rob commenting that was all he needed. It didn't surprise us when he threw away all his charge cards in a Texas lake while on vacation. I must admit that one was a hard one for me to understand.

As a young adult, Rob never dealt with depression and couldn't understand why others did. Depression must have been an unknown, scary place for him, but I never thought he would even consider taking his own life. He loved life, his family, and his pets. Satan's voice overrode Robs, and he must have seen sleep as his only escape.

In 2001, with the unknowns surrounding Jennifer's accident and the death of my oldest brother, my world was in turmoil. I knew that feeling of utter despair. I understand that desire to escape into sleep, but I only thought of it as a temporary refuge, never a permanent solution.

2024~I have made a choice to honor my son's life, honor his love for me and his family. I will do this by sharing sad and happy stories. I have accepted the reality I will miss him forever; I will never get over him not being here, but I promise each waking moment I will try to move forward, taking one day at a time and sometimes one minute at a time.

December 2001~I resisted the morning light. Swinging my feet over the side of the bed, as they touched the floor, I knew that I had to continue with my plan. "Mama, I'm going to spend the day with Butch. I'll be home this afternoon."

My new world was now controlled by telephone calls, I always rushed to answer, never letting it go to voice mail. Today, New Year's Eve wasn't any different; pulling to the side of the road, I answered. "Mrs. Kittler, this is Doctor Zenn. Jennifer is experiencing numbness in her legs. I need your permission to remove the halo so that we can do an MRI. The halo pens heated, and she couldn't stand the pain. I called Doctor Barker. He gave me permission to remove it and said that the neck is protected by the bone fusion. I need your permission."

"Yes, do what you need to do."

"Mrs. Kittler, please return as quickly as you can. She's having panic attacks. I told her many times that it's safe to remove the halo, but her mind won't accept it."

"Give her Woody, the stuffed dog. Holding him calms her. I'll get there as quickly as I can, but it will take a couple of hours."

After the momentary panic passed, I quickly turned around and headed back to my Loveland home. Thoughts of visiting my brother stuffed away. Within minutes, my friend and I were on the road to the hospital.

Slurring her words, Jen said, "Mom, they took off the halo. Doctor Barker said I needed to wear it for six months. I can't breathe. This neck collar is stiff."

I wiped the tears from her splotchy cheeks. The two indentions in her forehead from the halo screws penetrated my heart, and it took every ounce of strength I had to keep my tears dammed. "Jennifer, calm down, honey. It's going to be okay. The doctor needs an MRI to see what's going on." I tried explaining that they'd consulted with Doctor Barker. However, the empty look in her eyes told me that the damage from her stroke prevented her from processing the information.

"Well, then, why did they put this stupid collar on me?" she said, and then she wept bitterly. "Are you sure my neck isn't going to shift and hit my spinal cord?"

"Your muscles are weak; the halo has supported your neck for over a month."

"No, it's not going to shift. Doctor Barker also fused it with bone harvested from your hip." She forced a smile.

The urgency of the phone call, then nothing, just sitting at the bedside waiting. They excused the delay in the shortage of staff because of the holiday. The doctor reassured Jennifer her nurse would always monitor her pain and adjust her medication as needed.

Jen pleaded with the doctor to let me go in with her, but he explained the test would take at least 3 hours and I needed to wait in the waiting room. Squeezing her little stuffed friend, "Can I please take Woody with me?"

The doctor said, "Of course you can."

Gently kissing my broken daughter, once again, I retreated to a deserted waiting room. After three hours sitting in the hard brown chairs, the doctor finally entered the waiting room.

"Ms. Kittler had a rough time lying flat for the duration of the test. Luckily, I don't see any new damage, and her sensation has returned."

I nodded as he talked, and then I asked, "What's going on?"

"She's got some big screws inside her. One of them could be pressing on a nerve. I've ordered more testing, and then we'll know more. Go home and get some sleep; I know that it's been a long night and that this isn't the way you wanted to end 2001."

If only I could scream and tell someone that my brother is dying, it would loosen the pain inside me.

My world was split again when Rob died. The Holy Spirit had whispered to me one night when Jennifer was critical, and Woody became an instrument in my healing. Twenty-three years later, the documentation of her accident remains an especially important healing tool for Jennifer. She can recall the residual of the stroke but still celebrates her victories.

The night Rob died, the Holy Spirit picked me up and carried me in his arms, protecting me that night and the following days. Now, when I cry out, I can't do this anymore; the pain is too much. I know a power I can't explain will carry me through this unspeakable grief.

I try to recall happy moments to replace the unspeakable times. Celebrating the ringing of a new year was never a huge celebration in our home. Chicken wings and stuffed cherry tomatoes were always on the menu; you will find the recipes in the chapter *Treasured Family Recipes*.

Although one holiday holds a special place in my memory, we rented a cabin in Estes Park and played the mystery dinner game, sitting around the table eating a variety of fondue selections. Mom and Billy shared one room, and Debbie and Butch shared another. Jennifer and Robert invited their high school best friends. My favorite room has always been the kitchen, but I am sure I didn't sleep in there. I know for sure I prepared the family breakfast casserole for the following morning with homemade cinnamon rolls. Not for sure what we ate for dinner one night, but Rob drafted a poem about our time in the snowy mountains and my mama's farts. *New Year's Eve, Estes Park Cabin 1996*, included in the chapter, *Through My Eyes—My Sons Verses*. Recipes are included in the recipe chapter. We spent many mini vacations in Estes Park, so I guess I can see why we eventually moved there.

2002~Not the way I envisioned my New Year's Day. I wanted the Estes cabin, life in the past, but this hospital room is my world. One thirty in the morning, Jennifer was finally tucked back into her own bed. Kurt said, "Heard it was a rough one. The doctor ordered a shot of whiskey for you, but since it's New Year's Day, the cook finished the bottle. So, let's see if this shot will do the trick."

I couldn't bring myself to wish her a happy New Year. On my way out the door, her hysterical crying filled the room. "It isn't fair, Mom. Why me? He didn't even get hurt, and because the police officers screwed up and didn't arrest him, he's out free. It's not fair. I can't do this anymore. The pain is too much returning; rushing to her bedside, I stroked her sweaty hair off her forehead, "Honey, you're overtired. Give the shot time to work. You'll feel better."

"No, I won't. I can't stand this pain."

"Jennifer, it's two in the morning. You've had a long day—close your eyes." I sat at her bedside and ran my fingers lightly across her forehead until her breathing became low and shallow.

I returned to the solitude of my bed, pulled the covers over my eyes, and hugged my knees against my chest. On that night, I lost the battle; angry thoughts hurled from my heart.

My phone's alarm woke me at five thirty, and I returned to my daughter's world. "Hey, little sunshine, have you had your black-eyed pea protein shake yet?"

"Funny, Mom. Don't think the peas did me a lot of good last year."

"Do you remember that I'm going home so that I can share the black-eyed peas, cornbread, and ham with Mama?"

"Do you have to leave? It was so scary yesterday. Why did my leg go numb?"

"How does it feel this morning?"

"The nurse was in earlier, and I could feel the pricks this time."

"The doctor said that the MRI didn't show anything, but he ordered more testing. He mentioned that you have large screws in your sacroiliac joint. That might have something to do with it. Since it's a holiday, nothing will happen today—you need to rest."

Reminding her that her dad would visit later softened the news that I was going home once again. "When I return, we'll do something with that chopped hair since the halo is off."

"Tell Darlene hello; maybe she and Uncle Butch can come visit."

I shifted from leg to leg, wrapped my arms around my middle, and suppressed my cries. "Remember to call me before you go to sleep.

2024~Here's a cute story. Rob was such a wonderful eater, a little odd, I must admit. When his money was tight, he bought a jar of chow-chow relish (his grandmother hooked him on it). If you are like me, you might not have ever heard of chow-chow. It is like pickle relish but is made with green tomatoes, onions, cabbage, and colorful peppers. Rob ate everything except black-eyed peas. He was always a child who never wanted to hurt people's feelings, so one day, when I was serving my Southern New Year traditional dinner: black-eyed peas, fried potatoes, and cornbread. He got up from the table to go to the bathroom, but I could see his little hand clenched. Yep, he was taking a handful of peas to throw away. I never served him black-eyed peas again, but we sure did get a lot of miles off that story. Years later, a good Texas friend gave me a recipe for Black-eyed pea soup, which has become our tradition now. I could never get Rob to even try the soup. You will find the soup recipe in the *Treasured Family Recipes* chapter. Sharing these stories of my family fills my heart with an indescribable joy and peace that I know can only come from the Lord.

8
Closed Heart

*"When the Lord saw her, his heart went out to her, and he said,
Don't cry."
Luke 7:13*

3 January 2002~A dark cloud covered my heart today as I thought about the removal of my brother's life support. The hospital beckoned me against my wishes. Mama said her final goodbyes and then retreated home. Deb stood on one side of the bed. I positioned a chair on the opposite side. Deb spoke softly, telling her husband that it was okay to let go. She thanked him for his friendship and his love. Her kiss rested on his forehead. I read from his pocket Bible. My eyes focused on the verses he had underlined. Mama's heart cried loudly for her firstborn.

Oscar Mack Tucker, "Butch," was born on August 1, 1945, in Phoenix, Arizona. Everyone called him Mack. To me, he was Butch. We had recently reached a point in our relationship where past hurts were no longer at the forefront of our conversations. We now shared a common interest—the Bible. Dipping into our past, I recalled the many late-night arguments about his strict, judgmental, and unforgiven version of God. Butch's answer for all problems was "God will provide," and it was spoken from his head, not his heart. My brother traveled treacherous paths, and when his version didn't shelter him from life's hailstorms or meet his needs the way he expected—he found fulfillment in a whiskey bottle. I was so thankful for the day he accepted the truth that Jesus died for our sins and that we are saved by grace, not by works. Butch then placed his trust in Christ, not the bottle. He'd accepted God's forgiveness and, most of all, forgave himself.

I slipped into bed. My heart burned that night for the loss of my brother. I picked up his pocket Bible. Butch's written words soothed my heart: "If men see or remember Mack Tucker more than Christ, then I have failed, for Christ is working through me. If they remember a man sent from God, I've done better, but if they remember God and His Son, I've done well—extremely well."

The machine that had replaced my brother's soft-spoken voice was shut off.

Oscar Mack "Butch" Tucker died at 9:20 p.m. on Thursday, January 3, 2002, at the age of fifty-six.

The following days are all a blur; I recall trying to order flowers for the service; it was as if I was frozen, looking from the outside of me standing at the flower counter. My mind screamed he was dead, but my heart wouldn't accept it. The flower-arrangement pages ran together, and the woman behind the counter said, "How about these? Would they make a nice arrangement for your brother?"

Her words freed me, "Yes, those are perfect."

I worried how Jen would accept the news of her uncle's death—they'd shared a special bond. My mind was torn between mourning the death of my brother or celebrating Jennifer's healing. I felt like I was an empty vessel—life and death had drained me. I felt that I had no more to give; if it hadn't been for the arms of God rocking me, I would have certainly been lost.

The small sanctuary was filled with loved ones, and beautiful flowers decorated the front. Robert Kittler, Butch's nephew, ended the service with a reading of the poem he wrote honoring his uncle, A *New Kind Of* Start. On Rob's sixteenth birthday, we bought him a used Camaro. His uncle Butch helped him paint it a beautiful candy apple red. Rob always admired Uncle Butch, so it meant a lot to him to share the poem he had written for his uncle.

I fought the pull to step back into Jen's world. Lingering in the shower, Droplets of water intermingled with my tears and bounced from my naked body as I slipped a plastic bag over my green funeral dress, trapping all emotion and switching into my jeans and sweatshirt. As I left the world of death and returned to my world of recovery, my heart closed and dripped with tears. But I knew God saw me no matter what world I lived in and whispered, " don't cry, my child. By the time I reached my daughter's room, my facade was in place—every sad feeling stored in my heart, and the door slammed.

9

The Puzzle

"So do not fear, for I am with you; do not be dismayed, for I am your God. I will strengthen you and help you; I will uphold you with my righteous right hand."
Isaiah 41:10

2002~The days away from the hospital gave me little comfort, but I knew I needed to return to my daughter's world to help her heal. "Good morning, my little sunshine. I know you'll have lots of visitors today, so let me see if I can comb your hair. It should be easier with the halo off."

"Mom, can I sit in the wheelchair to visit with my friends?"

"Of course—plus, it will be easier for me to do your hair."

She grunted and groaned and raised her hips the few inches required. Working fast, I tucked the sling in place. The Hoyer freed her from the confines of the bed. I freed knots intermingled with shiny glass shards and dried blood in my makeshift beauty shop.

"I thought all my injuries were internal. Where did the glass come from?"

"Remember me telling you the story about how the nurse cut your hair so she could staple the laceration on your scalp?

"Not really."

"Well, it took twenty-seven staples to close the flap laceration the nurse said. I assume the glass was from the broken side windows."

The girls talked and laughed for over an hour; Jennifer began to slur her words, and I knew it was time for her to return to her charging pad. Sweet goodbyes were exchanged, and when we got the limp noodle back into bed, the crying started. "It's not fair, Mom. Why did this happen? I hate life."

"Jennifer Marie, I know this is hard, but you're overtired." Kurt quickly delivered her meds, but his jokes fell on an angry listener. I knew that I needed to wait for the pain medication to kick in, and then my little sunshine would return.

Mom. I hate it here. I hate it when you leave. Dad said they still haven't arrested the drunk driver.

"Jennifer, the police will arrest him. He will get his punishment. He didn't ruin your life. You must focus on your healing. Leave his punishment for the courts."

"But Mom—"

"Enough. All I know is that you and I only have so much energy. We can't afford to let him control one minute of it."

"I just wish I wouldn't get so depressed. It's like something takes over me. It's hard. Sometimes, I think I'm a burden on everyone." Her sobs filled the room.

I tucked a warm blanket under her legs and placed Woody on her chest. I pulled my chair bedside. "Jennifer, hold Jesus's hand. He will walk you through this storm; you can't do it alone. Rest now; let the pain medication work. You are a gift to us all, not a burden."

When her raging storm subsided, I kissed her good night and returned to my apartment. "Was it the power of Jesus or the pain medication that softened her thoughts? How I wish my thoughts would soften. I cried, asking why He hadn't spared my brother. I prayed for his recovery. Should I have prayed harder or longer? A dreamless night didn't provide answers but reminded me that prayer connects me to a mysterious strength.

The day began with her first progress/planning conference. The room was filled with Jennifer's therapists and doctors. A doctor clipped several X-rays onto the illuminated viewboard, displaying images of my daughter's skull. The knot in my stomach twisted as the light highlighted the bars and screws. I looked away before my brain could count the screws.

Doctor Pena greeted each of us and then addressed Jennifer directly, "Jennifer, you're a complex case. You've had many complications, but you are on the road to recovery." With a pointer in his hand, he explained each injury.

You are a lucky young lady. They call this dislocation 'the hangman's break.' It really is a miracle you aren't paralyzed. I'm telling you this so that you know the importance of doing everything your therapist tells you to do. Even on your hardest days, you must push through the pain. Your progress reports show you struggle with retrieving the correct words, and your memory scores are below average. The swallowing problems are also related to the stroke. The report from your physical therapist is very encouraging. She thinks you will walk again but will need a cane or walker to depend on for stability. But she did stress that with the severity of the pelvis break, you'll be non–weight–bearing until it is completely healed, which is about another month." Jennifer's first conference encouraged a successful recovery.

2022~I wonder if Rob feared something more was going on with his health, and he was going to be a burden on us. Being a caregiver for a total care person makes you rethink your health decisions. Rob had a special connection with Billy, but he also saw the strain and sacrifice it placed on the whole family. Rob wouldn't want that responsibility placed on this family.

Rob didn't have the support of doctors and medical support like Jennifer had; she was encouraged to accept her life wasn't ruined. Maybe Rob thought the same way Jennifer did; his life was ruined, and he couldn't find his new normal. Rob was such a giving and caring person; I can only believe he thought his actions were helping us. When a person is suffering from mental strain, they do not process the world around them the same as others. We say we would never do that to our loved ones, but Satan speaks loudly and drowns everything else out. Without professional help, Satan usually wins the hunt. Satan makes them believe everyone will be better without them. We struggle with that thinking; being the ones left behind, our minds say our Rob would never leave us. He loved us all so much, he loved his life, and he enjoyed making us laugh through his little jokes and emojis. All I can believe is that November morning, my son was tired of MRIs, doctor visits, and a light in his head that wouldn't shut off. Thoughts he couldn't control. And dealing with pain management. Enough, he said, took control, turned off the voices, and shut off the light permanently.

Those words the doctor told Jennifer years ago, 'Even on your hardest days, you must push through the pain,' ring true for us today. If we are to move through this darkness and emptiness,, we must push through the pain and realize that our world has changed but is not ruined. This journey will look different for each of us; on some days, just pushing back the bed covers and swinging our feet out of the bed will be all we can do.

It helps us move forward if we believe that things will get better. Find something positive to focus on; for myself, two main things helped: having my daughter and her husband and Rob's children over for brunch. Emma had asked for some family recipes for her birthday gift the year Rob died. I found healing in making a cookbook for her. I have always loved collecting recipes, so escaping into my collection was healing. As for her dad's favorites, I would always tell a little story about each one. I have found searching for new recipes and creating new traditions shows me that life will get better. Cream cheese danish has now become a standard brunch item. Find things you enjoy so you aren't pulled under and tangled in the web of Satan's lies.

Also, I have found writing this book has helped me move toward the light. I love sharing Rob's life and the things that made him laugh and love. I don't want him remembered as that one momentary act of despair; he was so much more.

His youngest daughter, Seneca, her two cats and Rob's dog, Ranger, live with us and bring laughter and love to our home. I don't have a stuffed dog to hide behind, but I love playing with Rob's dog. I always loved watching Rob throw the ball for him. It soothes my heart knowing I am standing in for my son in a small way.

We search and search for answers, but they will never be found here on Earth. I like the words from a song; the only scars in heaven are the hands holding you. This also gives me comfort knowing Rob is pain-free, his happy self, and learning magic tricks from some of his idols. And, of course, sitting in his little cabin warmed by a roaring fire, sharing his latest poetry with Jesus.

Moving forward can mean different things to each of us. If someone tells you there is a time frame and a way you should grieve, you should question whether they have suffered a loss. The books on grieving are only guidelines and not roadmaps. I genuinely believe everyone has a different path to travel; it goes, stops, and backs on you. The worst is when it hides and shows up at unsuspected times. I know this to be true; it took me over fifteen years to go through the stages of my oldest brother's death. I had filed it away so deep. I know moving forward does take courage. I often think about how I would love to sit in a rocking chair on a farmhouse porch, rocking—rocking—rocking—rocking.

However, we are challenged to move forward to honor their love for us bravely, and we can't do this without trusting Jesus. In God, we find hope that He is the source of our strength and will provide direction. So, today, I choose to get up and write this chapter and place the fear of the unknown in the hands of God.

10
Straight Edges

"Trust in the Lord with all your heart and lean not on our own understanding; in all your ways, submit to him, and he will make your paths straight."
Proverbs 3:5-6

2002~Glossy eyes and a trembling voice welcomed my return. "Mom, I can feel the metal screw on my scalp. What if the screws come loose, and something shifts and touches my spinal cord? The doctor said the snapping of my head frontwards and then back again missed my spinal cord by less than a millimeter. What if the bars move?"

"That will never happen." My words of reassurance fell on closed ears as she embraced her depression. "I'll have the doctor check the area in the morning. Hey, since you're up, let's get out of the room awhile."

We traveled the halls and found our friends. It was good for Jennifer to see others struggling. Being on the brain injured floor was hard for both of us. One boy was hit while walking home from school in the crosswalk; his professional piano career was snatched from him by a reckless driver.

The middle of January began the struggle of putting Jen back together, hoping she would walk again. She depended on the mechanical lift to get her out of bed, and we knew she would have to master transferring herself out of bed before walking was ever a reality.

As I write this book and reflect on Jennifer's determination to walk again, I am reminded of a box of jumbled puzzle pieces. My husband loves doing jigsaw puzzles; sometimes, it takes months to complete his masterpiece. Each puzzle requires a different level of patience and commitment. There was a difficult puzzle he couldn't finish, so he boxed it up and donated it. Many framed completions decorate our walls. Jennifer never gave up; she faced hard challenges daily in the physical therapy gym, working with jumbled puzzle pieces.

Nancy, Jennifer's assigned therapist, said, "Jennifer, today we're working on transferring you in and out of your wheelchair without using the lift."

"I can't do that. I can't even stand up.

"Yes, I know. That's why the slide board will be your bridge."

With a heavy sigh, she said, "Okay, whatever. I'll give it my best."

"Great, first let me raise the table."

I positioned the wheelchair parallel to the exercise table. Nancy slid six inches of a rectangular board under Jen's right hip. The remaining twelve inches rested on the mat. With both of her hands in the holders of the gait belt, Nancy balanced my wobbling daughter. "You're doing great—just a few more inches to go," she said.

I locked my knees. I wanted to jump onto the table and pull the needed inches for my daughter, but I knew that it was her battle. Jennifer's beet-red face signaled she had successfully scooted across the open space. That puzzle piece came at a cost for Jennifer; the pain was unbearable, so we returned to her charging pad until she regained her strength. The hope of walking again fueled Jennifer.

The following days sped by in a blur of busyness, each day more challenging than the last. My legs rebelled nightly after pushing and pulling her everywhere. I was thankful when Nancy softly but firmly said to Jen, "Even if you can't use your feet, help your mom. Use your arms to roll your wheelchair, especially uphill."

Thursday's dark cloud covered Jennifer; she hated it when I left for the weekend. The appointment with the lawyer required Gary and I to leave earlier than normal. Gary assumed the monetary responsibility, and I shouldered the medical decisions. The medical bills had begun accumulating, so I suggested meeting with a lawyer I knew, Randy Lewis. Gary asked Mr. Lewis many questions. I sat with my hands clasped in my lap. Gary would decide whether to hire Donald or take on the financial paperwork himself. Their handshake confirmed the passing of the financial baton.

My weekend was over, and the upcoming meeting with the housing authority weighed heavily on my heart. I had to ask for a change in the hospital's policy. The two-night rule stated that if a family member was out of their apartment for more than two consecutive nights, they had to surrender the room. My schedule was perfect—I rode home with Gary on Thursday night and then returned on Sunday afternoon. As I sat in the waiting area of the human resource center, flipping the pages of a food magazine, I thought about what I would do if they made me move. Mentally scrolling through the pat-answers I hear so often—Christians say trust God, all things work together for good and leave it in His hands—but none offered me any comfort. Then I remembered the words of 1 Thessalonians 5:16-18 'Rejoice always, pray continually, give thanks in all circumstances; for this is God's will for you in Christ Jesus.' Thanking Him for saving my daughter's life loosened the tightness in my chest.

After Mr. Avery and I exchanged pleasantries, I took a deep breath and forced my voice to say, "My brother died." I explained the details concerning my ride schedule. "I…I also have a total-care brother, and it's been hard for my mother, so my extra day home helps her." I shared with him the advice Doctor Adams had given me and asked him to keep the death of my brother confidential. Now, two people from this medical world knew. He leaned forward and placed his hands on my knee. "I am so sorry, Bobbie. I didn't know. I don't have the authority to waive the rule, but I will take it to the housing board. They meet on Wednesday night."

"Thank you, I'd appreciate it," I said, then rushed to Jennifer's room.

"Good morning, my little sunshine."

"Mom, the nurse said that she's removing my catheter. That isn't fair. How can they expect me to transfer quickly enough?"

"Well, good morning to you too. Jennifer, you can do this. Think of how fast you can scoot across your slide board now."

The morning nurse silenced any more questions with a handful of pills and removed the catheter. Now, a new shape of the puzzle lies ahead of us.

Her rough voice hit each syllable. "Mom, it isn't fair. Why do I have to go through this? Now, they take out my catheter and expect me to transfer to the toilet or use the bedpan. I hate this. What if I can't make it quickly enough? Mom, what about the days you aren't here to help me? I can't do this anymore—it isn't fair."

"Jennifer, you're letting the fear of what-ifs get you. Stop it. With everything you've been through, trust me, we will handle this. We'll hit the bathroom every hour until your sensation returns." I took a deep breath and silently told myself that we could do it. But I also wondered if I would be fast enough to complete the task.

Jennifer's daily work schedule required patience and determination. Nothing came easy for her; each challenge piece was built on the success of the previous one. Occupational therapy was wonderful; they worked on tasks that required brain-and-hand coordination.

We spent the rest of the day racing from class to class and successfully connecting with the porcelain throne. She was weaker than normal, so Kurt helped me transfer her back to bed. Remembering what happened when the pain got ahead of her, I was thankful the doctor increased her medication.

Doctor Pena came in for evening rounds and checked her neck incision. "It still requires monitoring; a small spot hasn't healed." As he was heading out the door, he yelled, "Keep up the good work, little butterfly."

"Mom, why does he call me 'butterfly'?"

"Oh, I don't know. He started it when he was explaining your open-book pelvis break. I'm sure that working in a rehab hospital, he sees a lot of caterpillars transform into beautiful butterflies."

"That's cute, Mom. Do you really think I'll transform?"

"Yes, I do. Look at how far you've come. Sometimes you forget. Besides the accident, you've had two strokes and a bleeding ulcer.

January 2023~ Whatever was going on with Rob, no one knew. He didn't share his inner demons even with his closest friends; they were shocked at his decision; it didn't fit his personality. I believe that is why his memorial service was packed; his friends loved him and were also shocked. Rob always made everyone feel special; he loved making people laugh. Of course, as Red Rob, he scared a few customers during his ghost tours at the Stanley Hotel. But he was also a very private person; he loved a simple life. Rob had mastered most of his physical challenges. He was back to hiking in his favorite places, although his balance remained an issue, and he never rode his bike again. The emotional challenges caused him to suffer. I can't even share them as they were all hidden in his deepest heart chamber.

Snuggling with the throw made from Rob's shirts, a Christmas present from Seneca, my mind drifted to the differing reactions people experience when receiving traumatic news. The first night in Jennifer's trauma unit, she was giddy; others sat in silence or voices raised. I remained composed and focused, and I handled all the information that was thrown at me that night and the following months. I recall the night my dad died; my body shook with deep cries, and those cries surfaced. As I write almost two years after Rob's death, I can't recall any of the events of the night or my reaction to the news. I pray those memories never surface. I believe we experience traumatic news differently, and we all grieve differently; some sit in silence, and others loudly cry. Maybe denial has been mine; I feel an earthquake rising inside me, but only little tremors surface. Fear of the earthquake erupting and pushing those memories to the surface scares me. Little steps to acceptance, I found the strength to donate the black dress I wore to my son's service. I pray it will be worn for a happy celebration, a mom celebrating and toasting a new year with her son, a time I never will enjoy again.

I do get mad at God and question why He let the death of his dad filter through His hands before Rob ended his. Gary was the practical one, the logical one. Even though we were divorced, we had a good working relationship concerning our children. We didn't always agree, but with Jennifer, we coordinated with her care and all the decisions. I needed him to help with Rob's arrangements, and Jennifer needed him, although I wonder if his emotions would have controlled him and he would have also been weakened by the death of our son.

Rob enjoyed journaling. He often encouraged others to journal. When sorting Rob's papers after his death, he scribbled on his to-do list, "How could I go from a few credits short of receiving my doctorate to where I am now?"

2021~Rob wrecked his truck, the truck he called Fred. He doesn't remember how he drove off the mountain, but when he was taken to the hospital, he said to the kids, "Sorry I let you down." No one really knew what he meant, but now, thinking back, was this his first attempt?

A couple of weeks before he died, he texted, "I can't do this anymore." I asked what he meant, and he replied he couldn't afford the apartment; it was eating up all his proceeds from the sale of the Estes house. I suggested purchasing his house first, then ours afterward, but he insisted that Mike and I find our place first. He had even talked about getting a motor home and traveling around; he had even looked at the small house for an option. When I asked him if he had decided which way he was going to go, his reply was always the same, "I am working on it." I had no clue to the darkness that reply held. Rob, the opposite of Jen, held all his screams inside. After his brain surgery, the light bothered his eyes, and Rob's brain would shut down if overstimulated, forcing him to withdraw to his dark room. Now, I am asking myself how much was surgery or depression? Rob dealt with his fear by withdrawing.

People don't know what to say when their loved one takes their own life; it is hard to say to someone that it was God's plan or that all things work together for the good. Sometimes, all that is needed is a hug. I found it difficult to answer the question of how many children I have. A friend who lost her son the same way says, "Two, one is in heaven."

Reflecting on Jennifer's accident and the words written many years ago about how I felt during the death of my brother, that feeling of being an empty vessel—life and death had drained me. It was then, and it is now, being wrapped in the arms of God, that I found the strength to move forward. I always encouraged Jennifer to find the things she was thankful for, and even when she is still afflicted with pain, we thank God for saving her. So, it is great that God surrounded her with wonderful doctors and ministering angels. But I must admit, I still find it hard to be thankful for anything around my son's death. Of course, I am grateful God shielded me that night, and He holds all the painful memories that keep me from slipping into the darkness.

Months moved into a year, then a year and a half since my son died. I am shattered, but I am fighting not to break. A piece of me is forever gone. I will strive to put the pieces back, but it is more than a missing puzzle piece that fell on the floor; it is a piece that is lost forever. By sharing my journey, I pray others can move forward and hold onto the hope that life will get better and not break—shattered, not broken.

"Hope, "Aristotle said," is the dream of a waking man. It's one of the strongest emotions that has kept humans going since the dawn of civilization. It's a strong belief that things will get better and acting on this belief."

I am not sure if Aristotle was a Christian, but I do believe he is right; hope is what fuels and moves us forward and prevents us from breaking. Jennifer hoped she would walk again, and she acted on that belief and pushed herself. I believe that, in Rob's case, he just couldn't put his hope anywhere.

I cling to the Christian hope and hold onto God's promise that I will one day have a reunion with my son in heaven. That promise gives me the strength to look past this heartbreak and emptiness. The Bible is full of promises; another favorite one of mine is taken out from Hebrew 13:5. "God said, 'Never will I leave you; never will I forsake you."

2001~Jen's barium swallow study showed that her swallowing difficulty is caused by the position of the bars and neck fusion. With time, the hoarseness would fade, and swallowing becomes easier. Jennifer's new speech class was more than the pronunciation of words. It was made up of other patients who struggled with short-term memory and retrieving the correct words. The class encouraged Jennifer to work through her frustration when searching for memories. The therapist reassured her that the undamaged parts of her brain would eventually fill in the gaps. The classes drained Jennifer's energy; she commented, "I didn't realize how tiring using my brain is. I am exhausted."

I tried to encourage and remind her that the therapy classes wouldn't protect her from negative thoughts and that she must ask Jesus for help. "You can't give in to the depression. Especially when I am not here with you."

"Mom, I wish I had your strength."

"I depend on God every moment of the day—actually, every second of the day. Trust me, I am nothing without Him. You almost lost your lifeline; your spinal cord was less than a millimeter from being severed. Do you realize how small a millimeter is? It's reassuring knowing His cord never breaks."

The depression was really controlling Jennifer, and she questioned why God would allow such a thing to happen. And I couldn't answer it, and I still can't answer why evil and painful things are allowed to pass through His fingers. I called our pastor and asked if he could talk to her. I positioned the phone close to her bed.

"Jennifer, this is Pastor Kent. How are you doing?"

With a shaky voice, Jennifer said, "Why did God save me? People keep telling me that God must have saved me because He has something for me to do. So, when I do that something, will I die?"

"It's okay, Jennifer, slow down and catch your breath. God loves you so much; that's why He saved you. He doesn't expect anything in return. He loves you. No one knows why He does the things He does or why He allowed this accident to filter through His hands. But you must remember that He loves you and that He'll never leave you. The whole church is praying for you and your mom. Lean on God. Trust that He will provide you with your daily strength."

With a calm voice, she said, "Thank you, Pastor Kent."

I hung up the phone and watched as my daughter calmly cried and say, "Thank you, Mom. You must have called Pastor Kent. I really appreciated his words. Thank you for all you do for me."

Amy, an aide, popped her head into the room and said, "Shower time." She helped Jennifer transfer to the shower chair, and on the way to the shower room, Amy said, "I think you're strong enough to shower by yourself. Here's the call button if you need me. Your mom and I will be right outside the door."

"Bobbie and Jennifer returned to their charging pad, where Jennifer was for physical rest, and Bobbie was for spiritual rest. The ghost-enemy returns to haunt Jennifer. It brings blackness to her world, and then it flees for a few hours, only to return. I know that there's a power that can slay the monster. I saw it when she was talking with the pastor; a calmness filled the room, and the darkness fled."

2024~After Rob's short stay in the rehab facility, he did research on Von Hipple Lindau. The genetic testing didn't show the disease; however, the Social Security Administration recorded it as one of his disabilities. After his brain surgery, Rob dealt with a lot of anxiety and unusual symptoms that didn't fit into the normal box of medical diagnoses. Each new medication or test frustrated Rob. In my reading about brain tumors, patients often experience changes in their personalities, and I did see an increase in his anxiety and paranoia. He started having Seneca, and I checked for swelling around the incision site, rear of another tumor. With his unusual medical issues, he fell into the same category as Jennifer, a complicated case. This confusing information and lack of answers pushed him farther into the darkness. After the lemon doctor wasn't part of his care, his medical team tried to find the balance of managing his pain and anxiety. Because Rob wanted a quick fix and wanted to feel normal, he often would stop taking his pain medication. When the pain became overwhelming, he reverted to what he knew worked. This yo-yo pattern was hard on his system. Since Rob still struggled with hearing, I suggested that he go to the audiologist. It wasn't until after his death I saw the doctors' notes from his medical chart, "Robert Kittler also complained about a dripping sound in the center of his skull, also has a "squeaking sound" in the center of his head, which is very annoying he says but not present all the time. He was treated for a benign brain tumor in June 2018 at Rock Creek and later transferred to a Loveland doctor, who recommended revision surgery, thinking that they might have pinched a nerve, or the doctor damaged the tissue when he removed the tumor. But Rob wasn't eager to do so since the chances of repairing it were less than 60 percent."

After reading the audiologist's report, I reread the neurosurgeon's notes from that visit. The doctor explained the glue system instead of sutures was the common method for closing the scalp after a craniotomy, and it was possible he had a pinched nerve. Another reason I know they did something wrong during his surgery.

Rob was such a grateful kid, looking through my memory box of the little notes he had given me over the years. Jennifer and Rob constantly expressed their love for me but in different ways. Jennifer would pick out beautiful cards and underline the special words that meant something to her, and then she would write a personalized message on each card. Words of encouragement are her gift from the Holy Spirit; she loves sending cards to cheer people up, as she says, "just something to make you smile." Rob would make his own card on a blank piece of paper, often on the back of old envelopes or napkins, whatever was laying around. Both children relayed the same message of gratitude for everything I did for them.

Rob would often write," Mom, glad you are so strong, and thank you for all you do for me and my kids."

At the time of Jennifer's accident, I found strength by clinging to Jesus; He was my lifeline. This is my struggle with Rob's death; at times, I don't feel like I am strong enough to reach out and even touch Jesus's robe. However, I must reach out as I know Jesus is my only protection from the ghost enemy that prowls this earth. Satan is just waiting to devour me and throw me into that dark pit that took my son's life.

Here's a funny story, Rob and Jennifer did so many things together as children. When Rob was nine, he begged us to buy him a riding lawnmower, not to mow, just to ride through empty fields. I wasn't keen on the idea, but I gave in to his begging and never regretted it. There was a huge dirt field a block away from our home, and those two kids spent hours riding that lawnmower. New homes eventually replaced the dirt hills, so I sold it without consulting him on the price. Rob wasn't happy that I sold it so cheap. I tried to make amends years later for his birthday, and we bought him an old riding lawnmower. Instead of his sister being his passenger, Logan, Emma, and Seneca spent hours riding through our Estes Park acre.

My children had different interests and personalities, but their lives ran parallel many times. Playing in the dirt fields as children together, or their love for camping. Rob engaged in soccer while Jennifer collected strawberry shortcake dolls. But I guarantee you that the other sibling was always supportive when one was hurt or going through a challenging time. In their healing, each retreated to their own little corner. Jennifer had her bed (charging pad) she would retreat to recharge mentally and physically, whereas Rob retreated to his darkened room, his man cave as it was called. He recharged by withdrawing from the overwhelming events of that moment. And that is what he did that morning, completely withdrew.

I am learning to trust God even more when I can't see the path to travel. I know my life is also like a puzzle, and I must submit to God and wait for Him to place the straight edges and all the pieces I need to heal so I can complete my puzzle.

11

Jen's Final Piece

"In their hearts, humans plan their course, but the Lord establishes their steps."
Provers 16:9

2002~January ended with Jennifer mastering the slide board; February was harder than the previous month. She continued pushing herself to regain what the drunk driver had taken from her. She needed the main piece of walking to see how the finished puzzle would look. Being a prisoner in a wheelchair emotionally wore her down. She needed a peek into what the finished puzzle would look like. The doctor wouldn't risk her standing before the bones were healed. But at least we had a small peak. At her last conference, we were told that Jennifer should make it home for Easter. Every progress report had said she would be walking when released.

In preparation for going home and caring for herself, she will be moving to the east wing. Moving to the other side also meant I would give up my apartment and be with her day and night so I could learn how to care for her needs when we went home. The room has a pull-out sofa. Her nurse sensed Jennifer was afraid of change, and I was nervous. "Now don't look so down; a move to the east side is one step closer to going home. Plus, the occupational therapist even ordered a computer for your room."

"But…But I heard I'll have to do everything by myself there."

"Honey child, you're being taught living skills so you can go home; but you'll still have to come over here for the dining room and therapy. Jen, some patients never get the opportunity to cross the sky bridge to the other side; their destination is a nursing home. The aides will be here in a smidgen to roll you over. Just stay in bed and let those young bucks do the work."

"Mom, I don't want to go. I'll have different nurses. Someone said I'd have to do my own laundry. I can't even walk. How could they expect me to do everything?"

Before the morning shift ended, two aides piled Jennifer's belongings around her tense body and pushed her through the glass-covered breezeway. My mind questioned each step: Would she walk again? Would her stroke hinder her ability to return to her job of processing payroll, a job she has had for five years? Would we be strong enough to accept her limitations? How I wish I could see if any of the puzzle pieces were missing. I must trust God.

Excitement returned to Jennifer when she saw the room, "Look at this room; it looks like a hotel room. It has a microwave and a table, and there's your sofa bed. I even have my own shower in the room. It's huge." I loved the large windows, and the atmosphere sang "going home." Betty, Jen's new nurse, welcomed us, and her pink scrubs matched her bouncy personality. She popped in and out of the room all day, either with a cup of pills or just to chit-chat.

The night nurse, Aaron, kept her laughing; he would say, "Jennifer, if you say you're sorry one more time, I'm going to ship you back to the other side, and then you'll lose all of your shower privileges."

At day's end, I threw the floral sofa cushions onto the floor, pulled out my bed, and crawled in. The partial wall divider provided me with some privacy, blocking some of the sound and light. When the nurse came in every two hours to rotate her or when the morning vampire nurse came in, taking Jennifer's blood had been much simpler when they'd had the central line in, but no longer needed since the blood transfusions had finally stopped. My alone time was gone, and my night prayers and tears were silent.

With my new morning routine in place, I shoved my bed into its holder and prepared for the day. I tightly closed the door to my heart. Daily, Jennifer pushed herself through every new exercise presented to her. At each day's end, we retreated to our lovely living room. I curled up with a good book. Jennifer played computer games.

Jennifer's progress continued; they worked with her and taught her how to do laundry from the confines of her wheelchair. However, her anxiety increased. "Mom, when we go home, who will turn me every two hours? So, I don't get bed sores?"

"Remember, I'll be there; if needed, I'll set my alarm. I'm certainly not going to let you get a pressure sore. I think by the time we leave, you'll be strong enough. Look how much you've accomplished in three months. I remember the struggle you had scooting across the slide board the first time—now you zip across it."

"True. It is hard to reflect on my accomplishments when I don't know if I will be able to walk again; the unknown is a scary place."

"I know you were scared when we moved to the east side, but aren't you glad you're over here?"

"Most definitely. I was surprised when they switched my hospital bed to a regular one. Guess they want this room to be a trial so that they can see if I can manage the transition home." Reflecting on her accomplishments helped me remain hopeful even when I couldn't see the finished puzzle. I missed my little apartment. Jen enjoyed her weekend visitors, so the Thursday goodbyes became easier, and I was adjusting to my split worlds.

"Not the bookshelf again. I don't like the nurses on the east side; they push Jen to do everything. Mom would never let her struggle with getting dressed. I know she would never stick me on the shelf. Bobbie knows how much Jennifer needs me. I watch her struggle as she turns from side to side to get her stretch pants over her hips. Jen, please know that if I could leap down off this shelf and rescue you from your twisted pant leg, I would be there is a flash."

Transitioning into preparing to go home added a different challenge. Jennifer was comfortable with her routine, but now she is scheduled for her first outing to leave the place she has called home for over seventy-five days. As the day got closer to the bus trip to the Butterfly Garden, her anxiety increased. "Mom, I'm nervous about the first outing, but I'm excited to see the butterflies."

I reminded her of how important these day trips will be—a step into your old world. We turned in early after a busy day of rushing from therapy to therapy, putting the upcoming outing to bed also.

A new week welcomed us with another busy schedule; our first appointment was with her counselor. "Jennifer, the doctor is ready to see you. Do you want your mom to sit out this session?" the receptionist said.

"Oh no, I want her with me."

The doctor complimented Jennifer on how good she looked and asked about her weekend.

"My brother drove my Grandma for a visit, and she made me macaroni and cheese and banana pudding. My swallowing is better; I didn't choke while eating."

"That's good to hear. Plus, I see wonderful reports of improvement from all your therapists. Jen, today, please share your feelings. I don't need to remind you of the seriousness of your accident, but you need to accept the facts: your pelvis fracture is an open-book break, the most severe of fractures and the high-speed impact jolted your neck forward and then back again, missing your spinal cord by less than a millimeter. Tell me, how do you feel, knowing that you came that close to death?"

Quietness filled the room; she gasped for air and swallowed before answering. "I know God gave me a second chance." After another big swallow, she continued. "I—I don't understand why I didn't die and why this happened to me."

"I agree that you've been given a second chance. Jennifer, there is nothing wrong with crying and questioning."

"I feel so confused. At times, I feel happy. I love others and even love myself, but then there are other times." The long pause made me uncomfortable, but the doctor waited as if he knew that the silence would give her the strength to find the hidden words. I was barely able to hear her when she said, "I don't love life." And then she said, "I wish I could die."

The doctor said nothing, so I followed his cue. My arms folded tightly over my stomach, and they held my tears inside. Jen continued; her tears muffled her words. "I don't know if I can handle the pain. I don't even know if I deserve to be happy. This man ruined my life."

"No, Jennifer," the doctor finally said. "Remember, he didn't ruin your life—he changed it. You must focus on the positive things that you've accomplished. It's up to you. This terrible accident can't define who you are. The real Jennifer, who's full of love, strength, and courage, must show up daily. You can't let anger and bitterness define you. The depression will come and go—that's natural—but eventually, the depression will become less and less. Trust me, Jen."

Jennifer's hands cupped her tear-stained face. Her body shook.

He spoke over her sobbing. "You have a supportive family and a wonderful network of friends; those are the things you should focus on. Do not give the drunk driver any more power. Do not hibernate."

Jen looked up. She nodded her head in acknowledgment.

As we rolled over the glass-covered bridge, "Mom, the rehab hospital is a sad place. I promise that I'll fight hard and push through the pain."

Caressing the pendant that encircled my neck, I said, "You'll be exactly like this little necklace I purchased from the gift shop, a little stick man disconnected on one side, and then on the other side, it's put together. The lady at the gift shop told me the "broken man" dates to 1960 and is an internal symbol of hope for Craig Hospital.

"I sure hope I can be put back together."

"You will be.

The east side didn't even have a Hoyer lift in any of the rooms. I surrounded her with soft pillows and gave her Woody. Then I grabbed a warm blanket for myself and pulled my bed from its hiding place.

Jennifer was extra slow in waking up this morning; I knew the bus ride concerned her. "Hurry, Jennifer. Comb your hair. We've got to get downstairs—the bus will be leaving soon."

With Jennifer secure in the van with the other patients, we were off for our first outing. Jennifer's sweaty hand grabbed my arm; I quickly asked, "Are you okay?"

"The driver is going fast, isn't he? There's so much traffic—I really wish he would slow down, especially on this freeway."

I placed my hand over hers. "I think it's just noisy. Plus, you haven't been in a vehicle since your accident. I'd imagine that it's just a little bit of anxiety. That's why outings are so important. We'll be at the butterfly pavilion soon."

Her clenched fist relaxed after the bus stopped. When everyone was unloaded, the nurse directed us to the back room for the special tour.

As the Butterfly Pavilion attendant opened a small glass cage, she shared interesting facts about the tarantula. Then, for the brave or crazy ones, the fuzzy creature named Rosie walked up their arms.

"No, Jennifer Marie, I'm not letting that tarantula walk up my arm; that is one fear that I don't think I will tackle today. Rosie can walk up your arm, but no way mine."

"Oh, Mom. Try it. She doesn't even tickle."

"No, thank you. I'm ready to see how many butterflies will land on my pink top."

We had so much fun roaming the paved paths and looking at God's beautiful, colorful creations. We made a successful bathroom stop and then loaded back on the bus. Jennifer's hands relaxed on my arm, and we talked nonstop about all the different butterflies—of course, Rosie dominated our conversation.

Jennifer had trouble sleeping last night; it wasn't from the extra stimulus of the butterfly pavilion; it was the excitement of anticipation of escaping from the confines of her wheelchair. Today, she was scheduled for the standing frame. I didn't have to rush to wake up; she hurried me, "Mom, hurry—get dressed." Her one-sided debate raged on. "What if the screws come loose? What if I fall? What if I can't pick up my legs?"

Betty, the morning nurse, interrupted the questions when she delivered Jen a little white paper cup full of medication and blurted out the unwelcome news.

My tone deepened. "What do you mean, physical therapy is canceled? Do you realize how long she's been waiting for this day?"

"I'm sorry, but the orthopedic doctor wrote the orders wrong. We can't do anything before they're corrected."

Tears streamed down her red face, head down, and arms crossed over her chest as we continued our day. The minutes turned into hours. The doctor didn't return to the hospital, and the nurse didn't receive new orders. For two months, Jennifer had dreamt of this day. But the peek into her future had been denied. This was a huge puzzle piece she needed. Would she return to the world she'd once known or remain a prisoner of her wheelchair? The darkness of depression consumed her. I watched helplessly. The decision was hers—she could fight or give in.

After a quick phone call to cancel my Thursday ride home and to update her dad on the cancelation, we spent the day rushing from class to class in silence. I wanted to cheer her up and tell her that things would get better. However, I remembered that day in the psychiatrist's office—he'd allowed the silence.

After her afternoon nap, we dined downstairs at the special Valentine's dinner. Red roses accented the white dinner plates.

After dinner, we went downstairs, and laughter from the recreation room drew us in. The instructor said, "Jennifer, squirt shaving cream on the paper plate, and then pick your favorite colors." Jennifer massaged purple and red watercolors into the heaps of shaving cream. Soft purple clouds covered a small brown-paper bag. Gold braided handles were the final addition to it, and they transformed the brown sack into a beautiful gift bag. I helped my crumpled sack back into bed, knowing that one day, she would be transformed.

As she drew Woody to her chest, I stretched across the bottom of her bed. "it's been a long day, but I remember the day you took your first steps. Your dad was making home movies, and I was holding your hands. 'Walk to Daddy,' I said. Then, your tiny hands slipped from mine, and you took your first step. Your dad filmed your first baby steps; now, twenty-six years later, I'll record your first rehab steps."

Searching for all the puzzle pieces didn't come without many setbacks and disappointments, and tonight delivered another. Jennifer was told the doctor gave orders for weight-bearing exercises, but she must complete water therapy before progressing to the standing frame. This disappointment and fear of another unknown filled Jennifer's with another restless night.

"Mom, are you awake?"

"Yes, you are up early."

"I'm nervous about the pool; I don't have a swimsuit. What will I wear?"

"I was thinking the same; I'll cut off a pair of your sweatpants; you can wear that large black T-shirt."

"Mom, would you help me up? I don't think I can get back to sleep."

We were readying ourselves for the big adventure when the morning nurse came in. With hesitation in her voice, she said, "I am so sorry, Jennifer. The orthopedic doctor had an emergency. He won't be in the hospital today—the physical therapy-pool order is canceled."

"What difference does it make if he's here?"

"He needs to be in the hospital just in case you have an emergency."

Jennifer threw the towel on the floor and rolled herself out the door. I caught up to her and rested my hand on my sobbing daughter. I wondered whether God was testing us, but He doesn't test people. I prepared my heart for the emotional abuse that my daughter would give me. *Please, dear God, give me strength to shoulder her pain.*

Jennifer forced herself to participate in all her classes, and then we both escaped to our hiding places, not because we were physically tired but because the emotional roller coaster had drained us of our energy. Since it was Friday, we knew nothing would happen until Monday. It has become hard to think about what the future holds for my broken daughter.

Monday welcomed us both with the same routine; we knew we had to push through and accept what this new week had in store for us. I pushed my reluctant daughter from class to class. I silently prayed with each step that the darkness that held her prisoner would be broken. I didn't argue or try to make her laugh this time. I knew that she had to find her way out of the darkness.

Aron popped into the room, "Hey, buttercup, where's that smile tonight? This may help with your depression; we need to turn that frown upside down. What's Kurt going to say when he comes over to our side to visit and sees that your smile is gone? He'll have my hide and think that I'm mistreating you."

"I'll try. But I don't want to do water therapy first. I want to do the standing frame now."

Aaron took Jennifer's hand into his. "Buttercup, you haven't put any weight on those little feet of yours in three months. You must begin safely. Hopefully, these docs will get their acts together, and tomorrow will be your day."

"I know. I'm sorry that I get so mad. I'm just sick of this chair."

"That's okay—if I get my smiling Jennifer back. You're one of my favorites around here."

Valentine's dinner and Jen's frustrating only a brief memory now; excitement and nervousness filled our morning. Aaron was right; swim therapy day was here. Jennifer rolled her hips from side to side until her black cutoffs were in place. She slipped on an oversized T-shirt, then we headed for the pool. With my video camera in my hand, I recorded everything from start to finish as the therapist tucked the sling under Jennifer's hips. Once she had secured Jen in the poolside lift and hopped into the pool, she lowered the human basket into the warm water. "Jennifer, hold onto the side rail while I unhook you."

The physical therapist cupped Jen's elbow, and a volunteer secured Jennifer's right side. "Jennifer, I want you to walk slowly. If you feel light-headed, let us know."

Through the camera lens, I captured my daughter's first steps since November 24. "Oh my gosh, you're walking." The words that surfaced mingled with my tears.

"Jennifer, Now let's walk to the corner." Sandwiched between the two, she inched her way to the corner and seated herself on the little bench. The volunteer placed weights on Jen's ankles while steadying Jennifer's wobbling. "Jen, I want you to do jumping jacks while sitting."

Jennifer slowly moved her legs, "Good. See if you can spread the left leg a little farther."

Jennifer's face reddened as she pushed her legs through the water.

"Good job. Let's walk back." The lift returned her once again to the confines of her wheelchair. *Thank you, Dear Jesus, for Your healing power.*

"Mom, I can't believe it. I walked. It felt so good to stand up. I can't wait to call everyone. Let's eat in our room." She was an encouragement to other patients as her smile filled the halls.

After sharing all the wonderful news with our satellite supporters, we watched the video over and over before saying our bedtime prayers.

Two days of pool therapy readied her for the standing frame. She breezed through the morning classes, and after a brief nap, we headed to the gym. With Jen in place, Nancy secured the gait belt around her waist and slid the slide board into position. Jennifer transferred with ease to the standing frame seat. Nancy secured the bucket harness under Jen's butt and locked her into the frame. My daughter's face was radiant as the machine slowly raised her from the padded seat. Nancy reassured her that she was secure and wouldn't fall.

Nancy constantly monitored her. "Are you doing okay? Tell me if you feel light-headed."

"No, I'm good."

Jennifer's feet were barely touching the floor, and her arms were resting on the chest-high table; all five feet and five inches of her glowed.

After she achieved her goal, I pushed her back through the breezeway. Sunbeams emerged from beneath her red cheeks. I tucked Woody under her arm and slipped the video into the slot. Aaron stayed for a few minutes longer and watched the replay.

"Looking good, buttercup. Didn't realize you were so tall."

"Night, Mom. Thanks again for pushing me everywhere. Hopefully, I'll be walking soon."

"That's what moms do. You'll walk soon. Night."

The next morning, Gary joined us for the conference. We were encouraged by the reports. We knew Jennifer was still struggling with processing data, but the doctor felt that, with time, the undamaged part of the brain would compensate for the damaged part. The occupational therapist scheduled her to work in the office twice a week to help her transition back into working. Doctor Adams praised Jennifer's progress and reminded her, "Jennifer, it's a moment-to-moment choice—you must choose healing, not self-pity. On the date you've been waiting for, March twenty-ninth, you'll get to go home. Everyone is so proud of your hard work."

Doctor Pena closed the conference. "Little butterfly, you've overcome many obstacles. When you leave here, you must continue to push yourself in all the areas your therapists just mentioned."

"Thank you, thank you," Jennifer said as she rolled herself out of the conference room.

Humor became a part of our world; Jennifer could feel the screws through her scalp and often asked what would happen if one loosened. I told her not to worry, saying that I always carry my handy-dandy screwdriver just in case. It was nice to hear her laugh.

March held a lot of expectations and a lot of work if Jennifer was going to meet her going-home schedule. She had completed the required days of swim therapy and the standing-frame exercise.

March 29, the circled date, fueled Jennifer; it ignited her longing to walk without any devices. Daily, she pushed her body beyond its comfortable boundaries, and in the evenings, she retreated to her charging pad. During the days leading up to Jen's discharge, physical, occupational, and speech therapy filled her waking moments. The evenings consisted of scrapbooking. With the support of her psychiatrist, she was winning the battle of forgiveness and acceptance. I pulled out the sofa bed and released all my fears to my Savior.

For three months, we celebrated with others; we listened as they shared their stories of recovery. We united with them in tears. Each celebration filled us with the hope of complete recovery, as we knew that Jennifer's departing celebration invitation would soon be tacked on the bulletin board.

One night before our prayers, she said, "Mom, I know now that my life wasn't ruined—it was only changed. I promise to work hard when we go home. I think I'd like to return to work."

A big X covered March 29 on the calendar. She removed the calendar from the wall. "Mom, I can't believe it's finally here. I'm a little scared."

"I know. I am, too, but we'll do fine. The new rehab team already scheduled visits with us; since you can't get out, they'll come to our home. Delivery and setup of your oxygen are scheduled.

With anticipation and nervousness, I helped my daughter pack up her things from a place she had called home for over four months. Of course, Jennifer wouldn't hear of packing Woody.

Funny story about Woody that really happened. When returning to Jennifer's room, she yelled, "Mom, Woody's gone. He was on my bed." We looked everywhere; Jennifer was hysterical. Her nurse rushed in to see what happened.

"It's…Woody. He's missing. He was on my bed."

Quickly grabbing the handles of Jen's wheelchair, the nurse pushed her down the hall. "We'll find him. Let's ask housekeeping."

"Yes, ma'am, I cleaned her room but didn't see a stuffed dog."

"I thought that I must've dozed off. I was tumbling. Was that my sweet Jenny's voice? Oh, please, let it be Jenny. Hope filled my body that I would be rescued. Then I heard a burly guy's voice and felt a bump, and suddenly, I saw light. My rescuer handed me to Jennifer. She hugged and hugged me. I snuggled to her tear-stained cheeks, I was back in my bed and in Jennifer's arms. She cried as she called her dad."

"Dad, it was terrible. When Mom and I came back to the room, Woody was gone. I thought someone had stolen him. Everyone started looking for him. You won't believe where they found him—in the laundry bin. When housekeeping changed my bedding, Woody was wrapped in the sheets."

"Jen, that's crazy. It sure was nice of the nurse to look so hard at him."

"I know; she said that if it had been an hour later, the dirty linens would've been shipped out to the laundry service."

Woody was so much more to Jennifer than a stuffed dog, he provided comfort and a safe place for her to express her fears and anger. She was more emotional with the thought of losing Woody than the day she was told about her Uncle Butch's death.

2002 March~ The reception room was filled with nurses, therapists, and doctors, each of them saying goodbye and wishing Jennifer the best. Jennifer cried as Kurt and Amy, her aides, hugged her and told her she was one of their favorites and they would miss hearing her say, "I'm sorry." Aaron said, "Buttercup, I will miss your smile and wish you the best." Lois picked up Woody gave him a hug, and said, "I will sure miss you two." Reminiscences bounced back and forth—one person recalled the huge Saint Patrick's Day party, and another remembered d the fancy Valentine's Day dinner.

Jennifer shared how when she was in the halo and couldn't move her head, a dog named Lucy leaped up and put her forepaws on the edge of her bed. "I know it's strange but petting Lucy's cold nose was comforting,"

Gary said, "I love that today is finally here."

After the final goodbyes, Nancy pushed Jennifer downstairs to the double glass doors. Gary placed the walker in front of her wheelchair. Jennifer pushed off with both arms, stood, grabbed the walker, and walked to the car.

In God's timing, the puzzle was complete. "I did it. I said I would walk out of the hospital."

2004 28 May~ Three long years of delays, the court day was finally here, and closure was in sight. With the help of our minister, Jennifer had come to understand the difference between accountability and forgiveness.

My stomach tightened as Jennifer stood. Using only a single cane, she walked to the podium. She rested her cane against the walnut stand; her hands shook as she grasped each side of the paper and read from it.

Clearing her throat, she said, "I wanted to tell you how the accident changed my life. I will never be the same again. In the accident, I broke the top vertebra in my neck, which is a break they call the 'hangman's break,' and slashed open my head, which required twenty-six staples. I had an open-book pelvis break, two strokes, and a bleeding ulcer. I was in intensive care for a month and rehab for three. I have a titanium plate implanted in and attached to my skull and two rods going down my neck. Because of that, my family was told I would never drive again. I also have a plate and screws holding my pelvis together. I live in constant pain from the injuries I received. I can't turn my head all the way, nor can I walk far. Every day, I face new challenges. Your actions have also affected my family, friends, and coworkers, as they've watched me suffer and lived with the fear of not knowing whether I was going to survive."

She paused and caught her breath, and then she continued. "I spent my twenty-sixth birthday and Christmas in the ICU, which I have no memory of. Because of my depression, I wasn't told that my uncle was taken to the emergency room on Christmas Eve or that he later died. I didn't get to attend his funeral. Also, without my knowledge, my family moved me out of the apartment that I had lived in for five years and got rid of my car. I wasn't told any of that until a month before my discharge date. I missed a year of work, which changed my years of service.

"I also wanted you to know that this isn't the end of the story. I have gotten some good benefits and life lessons from this. I have a new outlook on life. I'm more patient, caring, and loving. I became a Christian. I have met so many neat friends because of this accident. I am now appreciative of things and thankful that I'm alive."

She turned her body, faced the young man, and said, "Although I still hold you responsible for the accident and the damage you've caused, I forgive you, and I hope that this has changed your outlook on life as it has mine. I hope that you've learned from this. It would be a shame if you haven't."

She retrieved her cane, walked back, and sat down. My insides trembled and shook, but I forced each tear to stay submerged. His lawyer pleaded his case. My heart sobbed when the man I knew as "the drunk driver" cried and thanked my daughter for her forgiveness.

He was found guilty of vehicular assault, and the judge spoke. "Seven years in the prison that I call 'the belly of the beast.'" The click of the handcuffs signaled closure and justice.

12
Rob's Pieces Wouldn't Fit

"Call to me, and I will answer you and tell you great and unsearchable things you do not know"
Jeremiah 33:3

Thomas Wilder wrote, "It's hard to turn the page when you know someone won't be in the next chapter, but the story must go on."

2022~ Rob Never had his day in court and never faced the doctor who damaged his cerebellum. I did seek out a lawyer to investigate filing medical malpractice against the surgeon. However, after many phone calls and requests for medical records, the lawyer said their house doctor couldn't find any evidence of malpractice. The doctor's office threw it back on Rob because he didn't stay at the rehab hospital at the recommended time. That didn't make sense to the family since the doctor told us Rob would have surgery on Wednesday and would go home on Friday. The surgery team should have admitted their mistake and taken some responsibility.

Rob struggled to find a path to return to his previous life and couldn't adjust to the changes that the brain surgery caused. His lost puzzle piece couldn't be replaced, and without that important piece of his cerebellum, the puzzle was incomplete. It wasn't the physical challenges that drained Rob, as he didn't depend on the wheelchair for very long, and he hated the walker. He often used his walking stick for balance

Rob's vision was never the same after the surgery; he was sensitive to light and constantly wore dark sunglasses. When his surroundings became hectic, Rob's mind closed, and he couldn't process things around him, forcing him to isolate himself. My artist friend sent him paint supplies and simple crafts in hopes it would wake up the creative part of his brain again, but it wasn't to be. The artistic puzzle pieces were lost forever.

Rob's brain tumor was removed in June of 2018, and his desire to return to work was crushed at every turn. For over four years, he fought off many attacks from Satan. Young bosses yelled at him to speed up at a coffee shop, the noise of the escape room was overwhelming, and then his last job, filling orders for a grocery store, wasn't fast enough. He was frustrated at every attempt trying to find his normal life.

September 18, 2022, was the last time we all gathered as a family. Celebrating Logan and Krystin's wedding. I catered the rehearsal breakfast brunch in our backyard in Estes Park. We will cherish those family photos forever. Another Rob story, he thought we could have the guests sit in lawn chairs and eat on their laps. Of course, coming from a catering background, we ordered tables and chairs. Every table was decorated with pinecones and flowers; It was beautiful. Rob thanked me many times for making it special for Logan. Shortly after the wedding Rob and Seneca moved to the Longmont apartment.

When Rob died, the family decided it would be best if I didn't go into his apartment and help with the packing of his personal belongings. The kids selected the paintings they wanted, and I boxed the remaining ones and stored them in my garage with his magic tricks and books. Packing Rob's beautiful paintings was heartbreaking, knowing they would never hang on his walls again. His material belongings may be donated or boxed up. Nonetheless, all the wonderful memories we have made and the love we shared will forever be cherished. We will never box up the love we have for him. Even though Rob's nonessentials were donated, we found it difficult to let go of his clothes, as he had just purchased some new pants and shirts for his new job. Rob was excited about returning to coaching soccer, a sport he loved. We will never know why he did what he did that early Saturday morning, but I believe Satan whispered lies and filled him with self-doubt, and he couldn't face the possibility of one more failed job.

I don't understand God's way; even when I drifted from him and didn't deserve his grace or mercy, he gave it so freely anyway. I have tried to trust and believe his promises even when I couldn't see the path. Why didn't God intervene that morning and give Rob a dream to hold onto, a light into the darkness, or anything he needed to push forward one more day? If God did, but Rob just couldn't hear. I have had moments of being mad at God and even Rob. When Rob first died, I told myself I must wait until I get to heaven to ask him why he left us. However, knowing the reason wouldn't erase this deep emptiness in my heart. I realized that since heaven is full of love and is pain-free, the reasons won't matter. I find solace in knowing Rob is with God and free from pain and despair. So, I wait for God to call me home, and then I will hug my son and tell him how much I love him.

Whether you are a believer or not, confusion can arise about how a loving God can allow so much pain. I questioned how He could allow this. It is hard for the survivors; we search for answers that can never be found. We replay all of our last conversations or feel guilty we didn't have that many conversations. My answers never came in the form I wanted. I wanted God to put it in bullet points. Despite His silence, I believe God did not plan for a drunk driver to hurt my daughter or a tumor to invade my son's brain. It wasn't God's plan for my son of forty-five to take his own life.

I still call to God, asking for a small glimpse of my son in heaven sitting with Him, but He hasn't given me that peak. However, in my search for answers through these pages, God did more than hold my hand; He guided me and picked me up when I didn't think I could move forward, and my faith got me through the blanket of sorrow. I am filled with the hope and the promise that I will one day reunite with my son in heaven.

As you come to the end of *Shattered Not Broken,* I pray that you came face to face with the wonders of God and saw that His power kept me from breaking. Call to God, and you will find rest in your weary soul. Our hearts may be shattered, but we are not broken; we continue to see hope as we move forward toward the light, which is what Rob wants from us.

> *"Come to me, all you who are weary and burdened. And I will give you rest. Take my yoke upon you and learn from me, for I am gentle and humble in heart, and you will find rest for your souls For my yoke is easy and my burden is light."*
> *Matthew 11:28-30*

Through My Eyes:
My Son's Verses

Excerpts and complete poems were written by Robert Kittler for special occasions or taken from his book, *Can't Sleep Count Sheep* and his *Devotional Calendar of Spirituality*.

<u>The Final Answer</u>
No matter, no what, no whys?
No questions asked.
No answers found.
Why a million askings?
What for a few, truth what masking's?
Why we ask for never does it last.
It always beats a path of ours or down our past.
No questions will have the correct phrase.
For what no one will ask-outly stretched.
Upon the trace a tease upon the ask
Nothing empty long time lasts.

<u>Poetry Anthology (Beginning)</u>
In this assignment, the one you have asked, I finish,
it complete, and I did the task.
The book you read is mine, of course,
the words flow so smooth, I never had to force.
When I write, I am inspired,
if I sleep, sometimes I'm tired.
If I drink coffee, I
seem to get wired.
Plug into my writing by choice,
it's inspiring, grace and joyous.
For me, to write is to breathe,
for me, to write is the way.
write poems for you and poems for me,
some you know, some you'll never see.

Open The Door Inward
The closed flower waited and wished
For the time it was to open and spread.
The petals wrapped, tired and timed.
Patient it was, waiting to open to open
It will be soon.

Nothingness
I want to escape the noise
Bring me a second of silence
One that will come at a time
In a place in which the brilliance
Of God—hear this—listen
Nothingness

Time is But the Stream That Flows
The time is so close, so near, so
Here it is,
I see the window of blessing in the way
The week in which the day sits as the years go
Look around, inward you may
Seek only God in all you will grow
Love and know this is all you should know

Bees in the Trees

Along with the bees that live in the trees,
For the mouse that said, please, oh please, give me some cheese.
Cheese, oh please, please don't leave,
Ahchoo, ahchoo, oops, I sneezed.
No cheese for you; you're allergic to cheese.
That was not me. That was the bee.
The bee in the tree could not sneeze.
The mouse, oh geez, why did you tease,
It's funny you ask, yes, I do have knees.
No, I asked why did you sneeze,
It's not the bee in the tree,
But the color of the cheese
Please, oh please, take that cheese,
Throw that cheese into that tree.
Now you will see that I won't sneeze.
The cheese is green, now I won't' sneeze,
Now I have three colored cheeses.

<u>New Year's Eve Estes Park Cabin</u>
New Year's Eve, a Time of Day,
New Year's Eve, a Time of Night
In a cabin, We Will Lay,
Around The Fire, We Will Pray
As We Leave Della Will Sleep,
As We Sleep, Mice Will Creep
Bill Will Snort, Snore And Sleep
Snow Gets Thick, White And Deep
Mom Will Cook, Play And Plan
Della's Constipated,
I Think She's Sick
The Cabins Big. Made Of Wood
Ex-lax Would Work,
I Think She Could
All We Do Is Eat And Sleep,
As We Sleep, Snow Gets Deep
Della Would Give Anything If She Could Fart,
Champagne Leaves A Taste I Call Tart
It's Almost Time To Ring In The New Year,
Bill Seems Thirsty, Give Him A Beer
Everyone Tired, Fat and Full,
Pillows Are Fluffy Made Of Wool
New Years A Time Of Resolution Making,
Not A Time Of Resolution Breaking
Making Wishes, Not Doing Dishes,
But we should wake up early and fulfill our wishes.

A New Kind OF Start
Dedicated to my Uncle Butch
When I was young, I had a riding lawn mower
That would not start.
Butch knew what was wrong; he knew the right
Part.
He bought some spray and some gunk from Kmart.
Spray after spray on that little rusty
Part
Provided a jump start to my pretend go-kart.
You give Butch lemons, he could make
Lemonade.
If you gave Butch a hammer, some wood, and
Nails on a sunny day,
He would build you a deck, gazebo, or porch
Painted gray on virtually the very next
Day.
God gave Butch life; he gave it away.
He would do anything for anybody—this was
His way.
A man with many skills who would never
Present you with a bill.
He had a heart that was filled with God's great
And everlasting will.
A man of his talents, a man of his word,
Wings of a feather, wings on a bird.
The soul of a body, what's within your
Heart,
Your everlasting, infinite life has just
Begun to start.
Today, we are faced with a new kind of start.
We must persevere with the feelings within
Our hearts.
For his soul has a new start,
As he is in heaven
And always in our hearts.
God bless you, Butch,

Grandmother

With open arms and helpful hands,
my grandmother has many fans.
with a heart to give and a soul to lend
my grandmother has a sock to mend.
with the memories she's seen from present to teen,
I shall rate her the number one queen.
with a cig to loan or a voice for a tone,
my grandma can always be reached by phone.
with her age adding up and respect still the same,
I shall always be the fortunate of her fame.
with grandkids so old and booked to unfold,
My grandma will always have a story to be told.
as Della, I call her,
for others, I shall holler.
as my grandma stands,
as a loved one, she stays.
For she shall always have fans
and always know the way.
Through the good and the bad,
throughout this deep and shallow.
from the grass so green and the sky so blue,
Grandma, I will always love you.

Tribute To Mom (Excerpt)

For your birthday this year,
You wanted something sincere.
A rhyme, story or maybe a poem,
Something delightful your ears could hear
A bio, a digest, a story that's sincere,
A story of me, from here to there.
I will do this; I'll write you a story that is just right,
A tribute to you that will be out of sight.
Let's start from day one,
I came out with a cry but a cute little smile.
Never did I know that I would grow and learn,
Never did I know life is like a candle; oh, how fast it will burn.
You taught me so much in such a great, wonderful way,
There was never a day that I saw it some way.
How hard you worked,
To provide for us each day.
Or remember those nights, those great meals you cooked,
I would insist that my friends eat quickly and booked.
Sorry so much, but the food was so good,
If only we were older, we would stay longer.
You never knew how great you were,
And you'll never know how sincere you are.
From early on to later on,
You were always just right on!
Always there for us, with a smile,
Always there for us for a while.
Love you Mom

Home Inside My Heart (Excerpts)
At times, I feel I am right; At times, I feel I am wrong
Our family is strong, Muscular and mighty,
The youngest writes songs. The oldest pierces the wrongs,
And me, well, I see no wrongs,
Our parents are loved so truly and kind. They make a perfect match; they mix, they bind.
My mother is warm, old and new; she will take care of us when we feel blue
She cooks, cleans, and sets the stage, Always willing to turn the page
Dream, scream, fly, oh my, As we sit, we lie, we die
Cats, oh my, hear the roar; look close, closer. We have four
The house is green and bold, Filled with dreams yet to be told
The kids are anxious, young, and fun. Never hesitate to get a job done
Jen is pierced, poked and strong; metal detector, falsely alarmed
Rob is impatient, wild, and crazy; He Sleeps all day. We call him lazy
This is my life, no more to speak; This is my life. I've reached my peak
To search, replace or even bring back, I have dreams of filling the rack
For me to see what's good to be, I search, replace, and find the key
The key to my life is the way to go; I find it better to sit high than low
To fulfill your dream, wish or hope, Know someone who helps you cope
The one who copes with me the best, Is loving, kind and better than the rest,
The one who helps me do it is warm, kind, and tender, too.
For me to speak to my family too, These are the ones who help see it through.
With gifts of love so big and bright, These are the ones we give me might
Which will always be a love inside of me

I'm me; I'm only myself
If you pass, leave, or never move
love your life, however far and long
life looks rich when you are the poorest
grow like a tree slowly in the forest
live every day like it's your last
make the most of it and have a blast
don't live for anyone but yourself
impress, seek, and please thy self
I'm me; I'm only myself
Don't change; you are only yourself
I'm me; I'm only myself

Poetry Anthology (Ending)
My job with my journals is to complete the empty pages,
day after day, and every single way.
Writing to me is my hobby, my sport,
I could not do anything else, any kind of sort.
To write is to live, to share is to give.
Partake in my book, give it a look.
The more we read, the more we need,
to fill our gap, to fill our feed,
of living with some inspired need,
I give you my book and my assignment to read

"May I always have silence as my number one companion." Dr. K

Treasured Family Recipes

Life is like collecting recipes; treasure the important ingredients of life and discard unhealthy ones. Never be afraid of adjusting to the changing seasons of your life. Sharing a story or a meal can be healing. And, like my life, these recipes are not in any order of importance.

Catering

Wake up, wake up; I need help with this delivery
No, no, Go away, Ask me some mother day
It will just be a little bit; All you have to do is help me load and then sit.
Sit, sit, and wait till we arrive. Don't get mad if you feel deprived.
The morning starts early; the day ends late
I don't feel scrumptious If I miss my date
The dishes pile up, The floor gets wet
The radio is too loud, The air conditioner is too cold
Not feeling like I looked luscious s, The business should have been sold
That's not my fault, It's not my life,
Luckily, she's not my wife; She's just my mom.
A mother like you will always do
The things, the wishes, The love that you fulfill
The love you give, The love I receive
Makes me and my sister do believe That we have the best mom in the world

Chicken Wings

The most requested appetizer from when I owned Bobbie's Catering, and this is a recipe that doesn't have measurements.

- Disjointed frozen chicken wings
- Worcestershire sauce
- Sesame seeds

Place chicken wings in an ungreased baking dish with sides. Lightly cover with Worcestershire sauce. Bake at 275 for about 2-3 hours, stirring and basting often with the sauce, adding extra sauce when needed. During the last hour, let the sauce cook down, drain the extra if necessary and sprinkle sesame seeds over the chicken. At this point, don't baste or stir anymore. Poultry should always be cooked to the internal temperature of 165°, but I let the wings cook to 175°.

Bacon Stuffed Cherry Tomatoes

This was another highly requested recipe, Rob's favorite. He loved the filling, so he suggested using the Roma tomatoes; just slice them and top them with bacon mixture; definitely easier. When catering. I served the stuffed ones on a bed of dark-leaf lettuce

- 2 pounds bacon, cooked and chopped
- 1/2 cup green onion finely chopped.
- 1/2 cup mayonnaise or to taste.
- 24 cherry tomatoes (this is an estimate of what you need)

Wash and completely dry tomatoes, remove stems, slice a small part off the top and scoop out the seeds. Place tomatoes upside down on a paper towel to dry. Fry bacon until crisp, and drain. Dice bacon into small pieces. In a medium bowl, mix bacon, green onions, and mayonnaise. Using a small spoon or scoop, fill each tomato with the mixture. Refrigerate until serving.

Fiesta Frito Corn Salad

Rob found this recipe in the newspaper and wanted it for his birthday. I just love that kid and miss him so much.

- 32 ounces of frozen corn
- 8 green onions chopped.
- One red, green and orange bell pepper, chopped.
- 8 ounces of sour cream,
- 8 ounces mayonnaise
- One envelope of original buttermilk dip or fiesta dip
- 16 ounces of chili-cheese Fritos

Dice green onions and bell peppers. Place in the large mixing bowl, and refrigerate covered. Mix the sour cream, mayo, and dry dip mix. Add the frozen corn to the chopped onion/pepper mixture. Stir in the dressing mixture. Refrigerator until serving, and just before serving, stir in the Fritos. I make mine with sixteen ounces of sour cream instead of sour cream and mayonnaise mixture.

Black-Eyed Pea Soup

I love doing this for New Year's Day. This recipe was given to me by my childhood friend, Debbie. Jennifer loves this recipe, but Rob hates peas.

- 1-pound black-eyed peas, dried
- 12 slices bacon, cubed.
- 3 medium potatoes, cubed.
- 1 large onion, chopped.
- 2 cans diced tomatoes with green chilies.
- 1/2 teaspoon tabasco sauce
- 1 1/2 teaspoons Worcestershire sauce

Wash the peas per direction and place them in a slow cooker. Cover with water plenty of water. Seasoned with salt and pepper. Adjust the temperature to the lowest setting and cook overnight. The next morning, sauté bacon, add potatoes and onions and cook until onions are soft. Drain any grease, add to slow cooker, and stir in the canned tomatoes and spices. s Continuing cooking on low for 4-5 hours.

Breakfast Casserole

I make this every Christmas for breakfast, a childhood favorite of Jen's and Rob's. Now, it has become the number one favorite for my brunches. Preparing the night before and cooking the next day is what makes this recipe one of my favorites.

- 12 eggs
- 24 ounces frozen diced potatoes with onions and green pepper, thawed
- Salt and pepper to taste, ¼ teaspoon of dry mustard, optional
- 1 pound breakfast sausage
- 1 cup diced ham or bacon or a mixture
- 2 cups milk. You can make it richer by using part half and half.
- 1 small onion, chopped
- 1/2 cups Colby Monterey jack cheese, shredded
- 1 to 1-1/2 cups cheddar cheese, shredded
- 4 ounces diced green chiles drained or mushrooms

This is a recipe you can tailor to your family; I don't like mushrooms, so I use green chilies, and I leave out the dry mustard.

In a large skillet, cook sausage and onion until thoroughly cooked, drain. Grease a 9x15 glass pan, spread potatoes, and sprinkle with spices. In a large bowl, whisk the eggs, milk, and cheese. Add the meat of your choice and any other ingredients you like. Pour over potatoes, cover with foil, and refrigerate overnight. Bake uncovered at 350 degrees for 90-120 minutes or until a knife inserted comes out clean.

Cinnamon Rolls

I love this recipe. I hesitated to use the cream, but I love how they come out. Of course, you can make your own yeast bread, but I love the convenience of frozen dough.

- One-pound loaf of frozen dough, thawed
- 2/3 cup packed brown sugar
- 1 teaspoon ground cinnamon, I always add a little more
- 2 tablespoons, unsalted butter, cold
- 3 Tablespoons melted butter
- 1/2 cup finely chopped pecans (I personally don't add the nuts)
- 6 tablespoons half-and-half cream

GLAZE:
- 1 cup confectioners' sugar
- 1-1/2 Tablespoons milk or cream
- 2 teaspoons vanilla extract or almond extract

Using the cold butter, grease a 9x13-inch pan. In a small bowl, mix brown sugar, nuts, and cinnamon. Turn dough onto a floured surface; roll to an 18x12-in. rectangle. Spread with melted butter to within 1/2 in. of edges: sprinkle evenly with the brown sugar mixture. Roll up jelly-roll style, starting with a long side, and pinch seam to seal. Cut into slices. Place in a greased pan, cut side down. Cover with a kitchen towel, and let rise in a warm place until doubled. Drizzle the half and half over the rolls. Preheat oven to 350°. Bake for 20-25 minutes or until lightly browned. Cool slightly. In a small bowl, mix confectioners' sugar, cream, and vanilla; spread over warm rolls.

Banana Pudding

Banana pudding was a childhood favorite, especially Billy and Ashlee's. Looking through my photo album, it was awesome to see so many photos of all my grandchildren making banana pudding. It is still one of our favorites.

- Vanilla wafers (It's best not to use a cheap brand)
- 2 bananas, large
- Large box of Instant vanilla pudding and pie filling
- Milk per direction

I like using a glass dish so I can see the cookies and place the wafers on the bottom and around all sides. Mix the pudding per direction; after it thickens, crumble a handful of the wafers into the mix. Thinly slice one banana and stir into the pudding. Layer half of the pudding mix in the dish, top with sliced bananas and wafers, and top with the remaining pudding. Add more wafers around the edges, but do not top with any bananas, as they will turn dark. Refrigerate; this tastes best when it sits for a couple of hours to soften the cookies.

Chocolate Pie

From my Mama, Della Bomar. A big favorite of the grandkids.

- 1 each baked pie shell
- 1 cup sugar
- 1/2 cup Cocoa unsweetened
- 1/4 cup cornstarch
- 3 egg yolks
- 2 cups milk and a dash of salt
- 1 teaspoon vanilla
- 1 tablespoon butter

In a heavy-duty saucepan, combine sugar, cocoa, cornstarch, and salt. Stir in milk and beaten egg yolks. Cook over medium heat, stirring constantly until thickened; add vanilla, remove from heat and add butter, stir until butter is melted, then pour into baked pie shell.

Banana Cream Supreme Pie

A huge favorite of Rob's and a simple recipe.

- 8 each graham crackers or 1 1/4 cups crushed
- 1/4 cup butter or margarine, melted
- 3 tablespoons sugar
- 1 cup sour cream
- 1/2 cup milk
- 1 small box of instant vanilla pudding or banana instant pudding
- 12 ounces Cool Whip®
- 3 bananas

Crush graham crackers, place them in a bowl, add melted butter and sugar, and mix well. Press the crumb mixture onto the flat bottom of the springform pan. In a large bowl, whisk sour cream and milk until blended; add the pudding mix and stir until the pudding is dissolved, then stir in a cool whip. Spread half of the filling over the crust. Slice bananas and arrange over-filling. Spread the remaining filling over the bananas. Chill. To serve, remove the collar from the springform; this is a soft dessert.

Cherry Cream Cheese Pie

From my Mama, Della Bomar, made this dessert all the time, a favorite of Robs and Jens, and now Seneca says it is her favorite.

- 8 ounces cream cheese, softened
- 1 can condensed milk, sweetened
- 1/3 cup lemon juice
- 1 teaspoon vanilla extract
- 1 can cherry pie filling
- 1 baked pie shell, I use the graham cracker crust; I prefer the 9-inch shell

On medium speed, with the electric mixer, beat softened cream cheese until fluffy. Gradually add condensed milk and lemon juice, and vanilla. Pour into crust. Chill 2 hours, then top with canned pie filling

Carrot Pineapple Cake in Bundt Pan

- 2 cups granulated sugar
- 3 eggs
- 1 cup vegetable oil
- 1 teaspoon vanilla
- 2 cups carrots, finely shredded
- 8 ounces crushed pineapple, undrained
- 2 1/2 cups flour
- 2 teaspoons baking powder
- 2 teaspoons cinnamon
- 1 teaspoon baking soda
- 2 teaspoons vanilla
- 1/2 teaspoon salt
- 1/2 cup coconut
- 1 cup nuts, chopped optional

FROSTING:
Or you can frost with a cream cheese frosting:
- 3/4 cup powdered sugar
- 1/2 teaspoon orange peel
- 3 teaspoons lemon juice or orange juice

Preheat oven to 350°. Grease and flour a10 10-inch bundt pan. Combine sugar, eggs, oil, and vanilla, beat well. Stir in carrots and pineapple, coconut (and nuts). In a separate bowl, combine flour, baking powder, cinnamon, baking soda, and spices. Gradually add dry ingredients to the batter and beat just until blended. Pour into prepared pan. Bake 60-70 minutes or until the cake tester comes out clean. Cool in pan for 10 minutes before removing. Mix all frosting ingredients until smooth. Drizzle frosting over the cooled cake.

Mac and Cheese

- 16 ounces package of elbow macaroni, cooked and drained
- 4 Tablespoons salted butter
- 4 Tablespoons flour
- 1 teaspoon dry mustard powder
- 2 cups milk
- 1-pound Velveeta cheese, cubed
- 1 cup sharp cheddar cheese, grated
- 1 teaspoon Worcestershire sauce

Preheat oven to 350. In a medium saucepan, melt the butter, add flour and mustard powder, and cook for about one minute. While stirring, gradually add the milk, whisking until smooth after each addition., add the Worcestershire. Bring to a boil over medium heat while whisking. Reduce the heat to medium-low and cook for 2 minutes. Stir in the cubed Velveeta cheese and continue stirring until melted and creamy. Remove from heat and add 1 cup of cheddar cheese. Transfer to the casserole dish and bake for 30 minutes until heated through.

Blueberry-Cream Cake

A new recipe I made special for Logan's graduation. Now is a family favorite.

- 2 cups fresh blueberries, rinsed and drained
- 1/2 cup apple juice
- teaspoons cornstarch
- 4 teaspoons water
- 2 cups all-purpose flour
- 1 cup sugar divided
- 1/2 cup cold butter, cut into chunks
- 1/2 teaspoon baking powder
- 1/2 teaspoon baking soda
- 1/4 teaspoon salt
- 1 teaspoon grated lemon peel (comes in a jar in the spice area)
- 3/4 cup yogurt (I use Greek Honey Vanilla)
- 1 teaspoon vanilla
- 2 eggs, divided
- 1 teaspoon lemon juice
- 1/2 cup sliced almonds

In a medium saucepan over medium heat, bring blueberries and apple juice to a boil. Lower heat and simmer, stirring constantly until blueberries release their juices. In a small bowl, mix the cornstarch and water, add to the blueberries, and simmer until it thickens. Cool to room temperature. In a bowl or food processor, mix or whirl the flour and only 3/4 cup of the sugar. Add the cubed butter, cut in with a pastry blender or pulse until the mixture resembles coarse crumbles. Set aside 1/2 cup of the mixture. Add baking soda, baking powder, salt, and lemon peel to the remaining flour mixture. In a small bowl, mix the yogurt, vanilla and only one egg. Stir this into the flour mixture until incorporated. Spread batter in a buttered 10-inch spring form pan. (the sides are removable.) The dough will be sticky; just pat it down with the back of the spoon if needed.

In a medium bowl, beat cream cheese, remaining 1/4 cup of sugar and the remaining egg lemon juice until smooth. Spread this over the cake batter, leaving 1/2 inch of the cake batter bare. Gently spread the blueberry mixture over the cream cheese mixture, leaving the edges visible. Add the almonds to the cake mixture you set aside. Sprinkle this around the edges of the batter. Bake at 350 until the center of the cake barely jiggles and a toothpick comes clean when inserted in the cake part. About 30-35 minutes.

Cream Cheese Danish

I started making a new recipe for our brunches, and now the grandkids request it over time.

- 1-pound frozen bread dough loaf, thawed
- 8 ounces cream cheese, softened at room temperature
- 1/4 cup granulated sugar
- 1 teaspoon of lemon juice and ¼ teaspoon of lemon peel
- 1 tablespoon butter at room temperature

FROSTING:
- 1 cup powdered sugar
- 1 tablespoon butter, softened
- 1/2 teaspoon vanilla
- 1 tablespoon milk

Thaw the loaf of bread in the refrigerator. To prepare Danish, beat the softened cream cheese, granulated sugar, butter, lemon juice and peel. Roll thawed dough on a floured board into a 14x8 rectangle and spread the filling on top. Roll up the dough as if making cinnamon rolls. The seal ends together to make a ring. Makes cuts every 1 1/2 inches or so, about 3/4 of the way through the ring (from the outside towards the middle). Twist each ring on its side so that the filling shows. Loosely cover with plastic wrap and let rise in a warm spot for about an hour or double in size. If serving early, I will place the Danish in the refrigerator overnight and let it rise in the morning. Bake in 350° preheated oven for 20-25 minutes. Cool before icing.

Lemon Cake With Lemon Pudding Frosting

Emma's birthday cake is my favorite; I love the frosting.

- 1 Box white cake mix
- 1 small box of lemon instant pudding mix
- 1 cup sour cream
- 3/4 cup canola oil
- 1/2 cup whole milk
- 3 large eggs
- 2 tablespoons lemon juice
- 1/4 teaspoon lemon zest

FROSTING:
- 1 packet dream whip
- 1 small box of lemon instant pudding
- 1 1/3 cups half-and-half or whole milk

Preheat oven to 350°. Prepare three nine-inch cake pans with cooking spray. (I like to use wax paper to line my pans). In a large mixing bowl, add the dry cake mix, instant pudding, oil, sour cream, milk, and eggs. Beat on low speed, increasing speed until the batter is well combined. The batter will be thick. Divide the batter between three pans; the layers will be thin. Bake for 15-18 minutes. Use a toothpick to test; the batter shouldn't be wet. Let the cake cool for ten minutes, then remove it from the pans. Completely cool before frosting. To prepare frosting, combine Dream Whip, dry pudding mix, and half and half or whole milk. Beat at low speed, increasing speed as needed until thick and fluffy and stiff peaks form. This will take several minutes. Spread frosting between layers and on top and sides. If you want a thicker layer of frosting between layers, double the frosting ingredients. I prefer the thinner frosting layers.

Rice and Raisins

A huge favorite of Jennifer and Rob and Logan.

- 2 cups white rice
- 4 cups water
- 3 cups whole milk
- 1/2 cup sugar; add more if you want it sweeter
- 3/4 cup raisins
- 1 tablespoon vanilla
- 1 teaspoon cinnamon

In a large pot, add water, unrinsed rice and 2 cups of milk; bring to a low boil; when it starts to boil, turn on low and add raisins. Cover, add the milk as the rice cooks, and add the sugar when near completion; it takes app. 30 minutes to make.

Kraut Burgers

This is a German recipe from Gary's Mom, but she made the dough from scratch, whereas I use frozen bread dough. Hers were better as the dough was thinner and did have a different texture than the frozen dough. Interesting fact about Gary, his family came to the United States when he was five. Coming from Texas, I had never had kraut burgers until we married; they are often called cabbage burgers.

- 1/2 cup shortening
- 2 to 3 medium onions, chopped
- 2 heads of green cabbage shredded
- 4 pounds of ground beef
- Salt and pepper to taste
- 3 loaves frozen bread dough, thawed

Sauté onions in shortening till tender and pale. Add cabbage and cook till tender and lightly brown; you may need to add a little water as you go. Do not rush this part; you want to get the cabbage a light brown, salt, and pepper cabbage. Set aside. Cook the beef until no pink remains, breaking up as it cooks, seasoning to taste. Drain cooked beef and add to the cabbage mixture. Stir until meat and cabbage are combined, taste, and add more salt and pepper to meet your personal taste.

Using a thawed one-pound loaf of bread, cut each loaf into 7 equal pieces and keep it covered with a towel to prevent it from drying out. On a floured surface, roll each piece into a circle and top it with 3/4 to 1 cup of the cooled mixture. Beginning in the center of the circle, bring the two edges together, pinch the two sides, and draw up to the center. Press the seam down and place the seam side down on an ungreased baking sheet. Bake in a 350-degree oven for 25-30 minutes or until golden brown.

Resources

Three times I pleaded with the Lord to take it away from me. But he said to me, My grace is sufficient for you, for my power is made perfect in weakness. Therefore, I will boast even more gladly about my weakness so that Christ's power may rest on me. That is why for Christ's sake, I delight in weakness, in insults, in hardships, in persecutions in difficulties. For when I am weak, then I am strong.
2 Corinthians 12:8-10

<u>Each community has a suicide hotline</u>
<u>988 is the national suicide number</u>

If you are suffering from depression, don't be ashamed to seek professional help. We, on the outside, can't always see your pain. For us who are left behind with the hurt and unanswered questions, we must not let guilt take hold. If we do, Satan will jump on us and attack. I know for myself I have gone there, asking myself if I should have seen it, if I should have done something different, I quickly have to remember our good times together, and I will not let Satan tarnish those memories.

Grief touches each of us differently; the grieving journey takes as long as it takes, and the path looks different for each person. For me, isolation was my safe place. The two-year anniversary of losing my son is two flips of the calendar away. Writing this book was extremely hard and I thought about giving up, but then I would think of a funny story about Rob and that fueled me to write another page.

If you are faced with a difficult medical decision, don't hesitate to seek a second opinion or utilize the, Michael Skolnik Medical Transparency Act.

During the urgency of Rob's brain tumor, we trusted the man in the white coat, a regret I have for not seeking a second opinion. We have now looked up his record, and no negative reports have been filed in the state of Colorado, although he now practices in another state.

Everyone should have a person designated as the Medical Power of Attorney. Those forms are online, and each state's requirements vary. Rob gave me his medical power of attorney years ago, and I was able to look at all his records and help with his medical decisions.

If you are journaling negative entries or having dark thoughts, please reach out to someone. I know talking about personal issues may be difficult, but seek professional help. Please know that your family will not be better without you.

The final resource I would recommend is the Holy Bible and talk to God. Believe there is a path forward. However, I realized it takes me more than journaling, medication, or therapy to move forward through the darkness of grief: It's daily surrendering and admitting I cannot even hold onto hope without God's help.

"He heals the brokenhearted and binds up their wounds."
Psalm 147:3

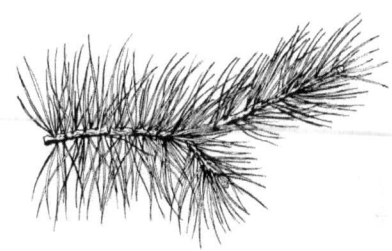

Photo Gallery

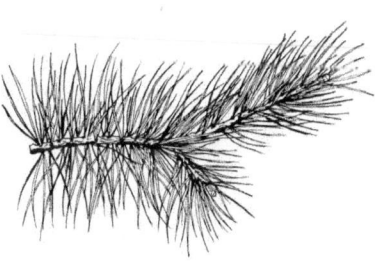

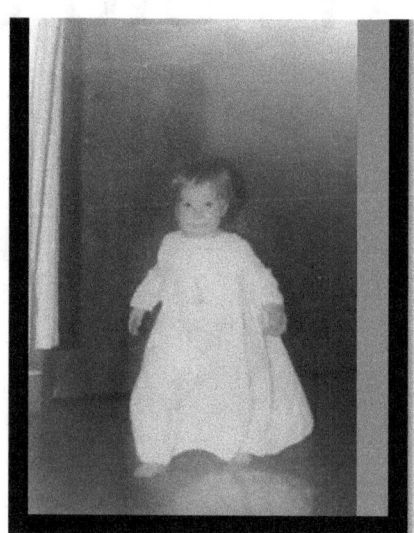

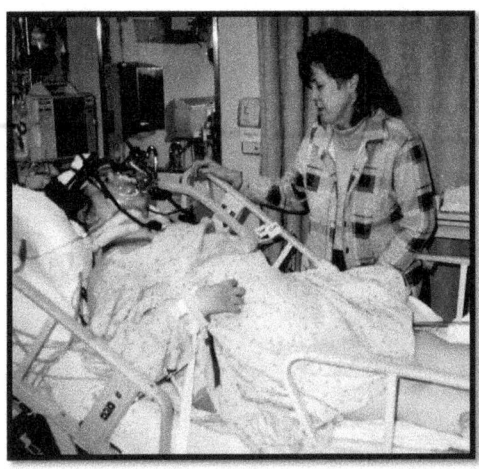
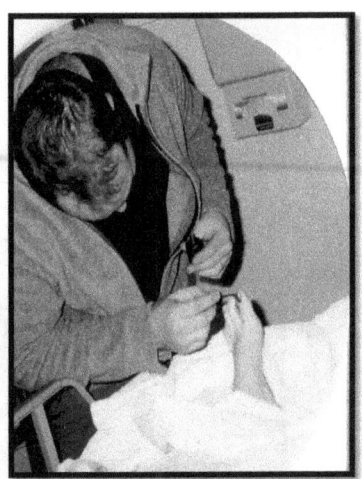
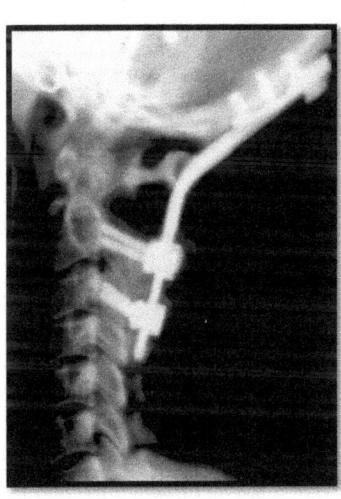
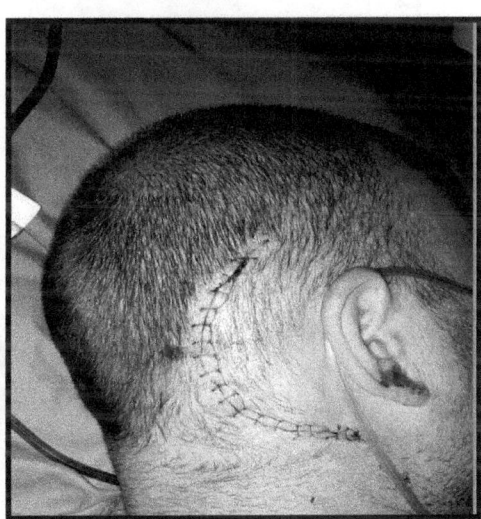

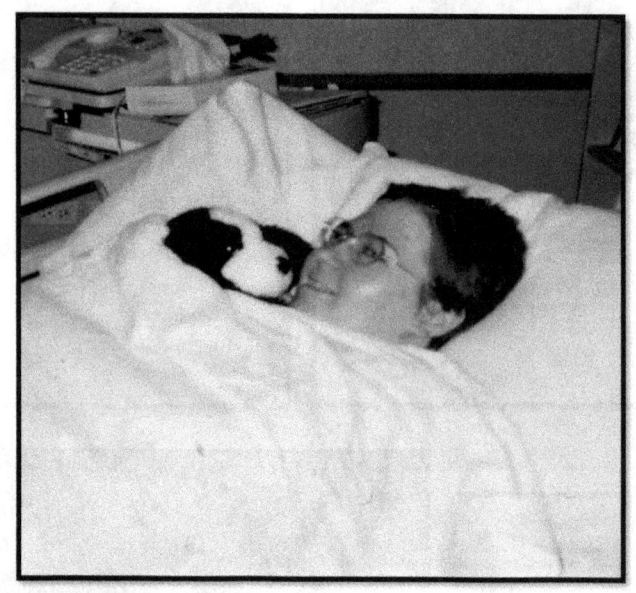

A Safe Place for My Grief

Dear God,

A Safe Place for My Grief

Dear God,

A Safe Place for My Grief

Dear God,

A Safe Place for My Grief

Dear God,

A Safe Place for My Grief

Dear God,

A Safe Place for My Grief

Dear God,

A Safe Place for My Grief

Dear God,

A Safe Place for My Grief

Dear God,

A Safe Place for My Grief

Dear God,

A Safe Place for My Grief

Dear God,

A Safe Place for My Grief

Dear God,

A Safe Place for My Grief

Dear God,

A Safe Place for My Grief

Dear God,